The Joy of Y'at Catholicism

The Joy of Y'at Catholicism

Earl J. Higgins

PELICAN PUBLISHING COMPANY
GRETNA 2007

*The word "Pelican" and the depiction of a pelican are trademarks
of Pelican Publishing Company, Inc., and are registered in the
U.S. Patent and Trademark Office.*

Library of Congress Cataloging-in-Publication Data

Higgins, Earl J.
  The joy of Y'at Catholicism / Earl J. Higgins.
    p. cm.
  ISBN 978-1-58980-410-4 (pbk. : alk. paper) 1. Catholic
Church—Louisiana—New Orleans. 2. Christianity and culture—
Louisiana—New Orleans. 3. New Orleans (La.)—Religious life
and customs. I. Title.
  BX1418.N4H54 2007
  282'.76335—dc22

                                                    2006103232

Printed in the United States of America
Published by Pelican Publishing Company, Inc.
1000 Burmaster Street, Gretna, Louisiana 70053

*For Bill Rittenberg, who eats
green gumbo on Holy Thursday*

Contents

Chapter 1   Where Y'at? 9

Chapter 2   New Orleans and the Perception
of Reality 17

Chapter 3   Geography 23

Chapter 4   Churches 33

Chapter 5   Theology 61

Chapter 6   Sacraments, Devotions, Holidays,
Feast Days, and Other Events 79

Chapter 7   Following the Liturgical Calendar 107

Chapter 8   Education 159

Chapter 9   Saints and Not-Quites 171

Chapter 10 Miscellaneous Stuff 193

Epilogue   Hurricane Katrina 205

CHAPTER 1

Where Y'at?

Where y'at?

The phrase is the essence of New Orleans. The salutation is not just a greeting. In New Orleans it is an expression of celebration and an affirmation of membership in the subculture of this city near the end of the Mississippi River, where the continent drains itself into the Gulf of Mexico. Hearing the phrase, "Where y'at," spoken in Pittsburgh, Poughkeepsie, Potsdam, or Peoria immediately informs the listener that a New Orleanian is nearby. It is a sound-mark of identity.

The phrase is a greeting, but it is no more a literal question than the generic salutation of "How are you?" or "How's it going?" The expected response to such questions is usually, "Fine" or "O.K." The greeter isn't usually interested in the fact that the responder is terminally ill, just learned of the death of a loved one, or has recently been fired. When a New Orleanian addresses a friend with "Where y'at?" the inquiry is at least as casual as "How are you?" The expected and proper response is not something like, "I'm right here," but a hearty, "Alright!" which is pronounced *AW-rite*. Much like two dogs approaching each other with sniffs and tail wagging, this exchange between two New Orleanians serves to identify each to the other.

By the last quarter of the twentieth century, the homogenization of American popular culture and language had reached New Orleans. The bland, flat Midwestern pronunciation of English that is featured on television had rapidly become the standard American English. Nationally recognized chain stores replaced local names such as Maison Blanche and D.H. Holmes department stores and purple-hued K&B drugstores. Idiosyncrasies in New Orleans culture were lost, as, for example, the use of the term "soda" encroached on the local usage of "soft drink" or "cold drink," even as older New Orleanians knew that the only use for "soda" was to mix with whisky. The once-common word "banquette" *(BANK-it)* is almost never used in conversation anymore; in the Crescent City people walk on sidewalks, just as in the rest of America. Use the word "gallery," and listeners think of an art store in the French Quarter or the Warehouse District rather than a porch on an old home, yet another New Orleans usage that has passed into history.

But "Where y'at?" has thrived, even resurged. It appears in print, a monthly local entertainment newspaper chose it for its name, and sometimes people wearing suits even speak it, although mostly with conscious amusement rather than unconscious ease. It may be that, like so much of regional American culture and usage, it will eventually be absorbed and superseded by the dominant forces of civilization, but for the time being, "Where y'at?" survives—perhaps a flash of exuberance before it is no more.

The obvious question is, where did the phrase come from and why is it unique to New Orleans. Like so much in New Orleans, the answer is a function of history. New Orleans was founded by the French, with French the dominant language for more than one hundred years. Yet

English-speaking traders and boatmen descended upon the area as soon as there was money to be made in the combination sea and river port. When Spain took control of New Orleans from France in the 1760s, there was resistance, some of it violent, from the French-speaking locals. Although the rebellion was subdued, the Spanish did not establish a strong cultural presence in the city other than the rebuilding of the Vieux Carré after the disastrous fire of March 21, 1788. The Spanish-influenced architecture of the French Quarter is one of many paradoxes of New Orleans. By 1803, New Orleans was back in French control, this time under Napoleon, who promptly sold it and a large portion of the continent to the United States. English slowly but inexorably became more and more important to commerce and government. The era of the steamboat increased trade and communication with the English-speaking interior of the United States. The Irish potato famine of the 1840s and '50s brought thousands of people who spoke a dialect of English that was very different from that spoken by the Anglo-Americans. As the nineteenth century progressed, more and more immigrants arrived in New Orleans from Ireland, as well as from Germany and Italy. The native French and English spoken on the streets and in commercial offices began to be affected by the newer idioms and rhythms of English spoken by the more recent arrivals. Also influencing the speakers of both French and English were the dialects and intonations of the Africans. Creole French and a Creole form of English could be heard on the riverfront and in the sugar and cotton warehouses.

By the middle of the twentieth century, a distinctive form of English was being spoken by the working-class descendants of these European immigrants. Their speech patterns in turn influenced the usage of the Anglo-Americans, the black New Orleanians, and the Creoles of color. Spoken New Orleans English appropriated French idioms in form, such as "making groceries" (from *faire marché*, "to make market"), and incorporated Irish working-class pronunciations, like *toid* for "third." The greeting of "Where y'at?" with its exuberance and implication of celebration became a mark of identity of working-class New Orleanians of all ethnic origins, and the noun, "y'at," began to be used to describe a working class person who spoke the New Orleans dialect. As the Old World languages slowly disappeared from the streets, New Orleanians began speaking to each other in the rhythmic intonations that have come to signal New Orleans. In saluting each other with, "Where y'at?" they had become Y'ats.

Unlike the larger American cities on the East Coast, which also became home to large numbers of Italian and Irish immigrants in the nineteenth and early twentieth centuries, New Orleans was too compact, too cramped, and too swampy to allow the creation of true ethnic enclaves. There was simply no room to expand into new sections of the city. Instead, the new arrivals settled into established neighborhoods that allowed regular and frequent commerce and interchange between ethnic groups. The Irish Channel is actually a rather small neighborhood, and relatively few Irish lived there. In another paradox of New Orleans, Italian—specifically Sicilian—immigrants tended to settle in the French Quarter, amidst the old Spanish architecture, and soon dominated the produce industry of the French Market, which wasn't French at all. The French Market was originally, and for a long time, a place on the Mississippi River where Choctaw Indians sold herbs such as powdered sassafras leaves, known as filé.

Filé is used to thicken and season gumbo, a dish that

epitomizes cultural mixture and adhesion. The word "gumbo" is itself West African, meaning "okra." The style of cooking, which begins with a dark roux of flour and oil, is French, although the filé seasoning is the contribution of the native Indians. A pot of gumbo is thus an apt metaphor for the development of the unique New Orleans culture. The combination of ingredients makes the final product more robust, more exciting than any of the ingredients alone. Likewise, "Where y'at?" became a common salutation among the people in this mixed culture. As years passed and generations changed, the many ingredients of the cultural gumbo became the traits common to all.

Common to most of the nineteenth and early twentieth centuries European immigrants, as well as the earlier French and Spanish colonists, was the practice of Roman Catholicism. A New Orleans Irish immigrant may have never met an Italian before coming to America, and he may have never heard French, Spanish, German, or Italian spoken, but he had attended Mass, the Latin liturgy of which was common to Catholics of all ethnic groups.

Because New Orleans was founded by Catholics, who have since remained the majority, Catholic immigrants in New Orleans were never subjected to the bigotry and rejection that was experienced by those in the large cities of the East Coast. In New Orleans, Catholics were free to express their religion easily and openly, without fear that they would be suspected of being subversive agents of an evil pope or some sort of junior devils come to America to corrupt the righteous. Just as gumbo bubbles happily as it simmers and harmonizes its ingredients, New Orleans Catholicism grew into a joyful and vigorous expression of faith and celebration that infects the daily rhythms of the entire city. It is written into the geography of the city and its streets. It is part of the speech patterns. It sets the calendar by which New Orleanians schedule their lives. A discussion of New Orleans Catholicism is not an excursion into nostalgia. The expressions of faith, worship, and celebration are vibrant, not merely remembered episodes of childhood and adolescence. Vestiges of Catholicism do pop up in the national popular culture, such as a long forward pass in football referred to as a "Hail Mary." A term in popular usage for admitting fault is a "mea culpa," even though most of the users of that phrase are not aware that it is from the Latin prayer of confession, the Confiteor, recited at the beginning of the old Latin Mass. Elsewhere in America, lapsed or former Catholics may state—sometimes with disdain, sometimes with fond memories, sometimes with indifference—that they were "raised Catholic," implying that they are Catholic no more. Even a non-church-going New Orleans Catholic or one who professes atheism or agnostic tendencies does not use that phrase. In New Orleans, Catholics who are born that way remain that way. It goes with the territory. It is like wearing a comfortable old sweatshirt or a favorite pair of tennis shoes. To escape Catholicism, you must leave New Orleans, and even then the change may not be permanent. In an essay in *Time* magazine, New Orleans author Anne Rice, writer of vampire novels, tells how she left New Orleans and Catholicism but felt the compelling need to return to both. She explains that being in New Orleans, living again in the city where she was raised, made her feel love for place, family, and God. Even New Orleans' most famous playwright, the brilliant, manic Tennessee Williams, eventually surrendered to the warm, soothing embrace of y'at Catholicism and was baptized after decades of immersion in New Orleans culture.

Catholicism in New Orleans is like the aroma of the sweet olive trees so prevalent throughout the city. It is sweet, ubiquitous, and persistent. It is reassuring; it embraces you sensually; it is impossible to avoid. Even people who are not Catholic are Catholic. A prominent New Orleans lawyer, William Rittenberg, a life-long resident of the city who learned the Jewish traditions at Temple Sinai on St. Charles Avenue, once explained simply and cheerfully with a broad grin of exaggeration that, "In New Orleans, even the Jews are Catholic." After all, the city's most elegant boulevard is named for a Catholic saint, St. Charles, and it is the address of two synagogues but only one Catholic church. The joyous, expansive practice of New Orleans-style Catholicism goes along with the exuberant greeting of "Where y'at?" Indeed, it could be said that being a y'at is being a Catholic, at least in form.

The Second Ecumenical Council of the Vatican, popularly known as Vatican II, took place in the 1960s and brought many changes to the nearly two thousand-year-old Roman Catholic Church. One of these changes was the use of the vernacular, the local language, in the liturgy. Catholics who grew up hearing Mass in Latin began to hear the prayers in English. In keeping with the Vatican II policy of using the vernacular in ecclesial matters, the discussion of New Orleans Catholicism in this book will provide the appropriate guides to pronunciation and translation into correct y'at usage.

New Orleanians are known for their ability to mispronounce street names properly. For example, the street named for the Greek muse of dance, Terpsichore, is pronounced *TERP-see-coar*. The French Quarter street named for the French town with the magnificent cathedral, Chartres, is pronounced *CHAW-tuz*. Therefore, to be true and authentic to y'at Catholicism, this book will also be a guide to pronunciation explanations of the local usage.

The y'at idiom appears mostly in speech, in the complex intonations, pauses, and stresses of the spoken word. Occasionally, however, it appears in print, as on the bumper stickers popular with anti-abortion y'at Catholics: "Ya mama was pro-life, Dawlin'." Those who seek to keep abortion legal have yet to come up with a bumper sticker to respond.

This collection of the practices and history of New Orleans Catholicism is not intended to be a comprehensive study of all that is special and unique about being a Catholic in the Crescent City. Instead, like Mardi Gras, it is a celebration of what is joyful and fun in the religious culture that is so deeply imprinted into the metropolitan area that it is impossible to avoid or to ignore. The greeting of "Where y'at!" is a statement of shared exuberance, warmth, and optimism. In July 2002, World Youth Day, a convention of Catholic young people, was held in Toronto, Canada. The big event of the conference was an appearance by Pope John Paul II. As the Holy Father looked out over the crowd of teenagers and young adults cheering and yelling like they were at a rock music concert, he may have seen a sign raised by young Catholics from New Orleans. The sign read, "Where y'at, J.P. II!" The pope should have been flattered to have been greeted as though he were from the Crescent City.

The old Latin Mass began with the prayers at the foot of the altar. The priest would say, *"Introibo ad altare Dei,"* "I will enter into the altar of God." To which the kneeling altar boy would respond, *"Ad Deum qui laetificat juventutem meam,"* "To God who gives joy to my youth." That joy of celebrating and living Catholicism is very much alive in New Orleans, long after the Latin has been dropped from use.

CHAPTER 2

New Orleans and the Perception of Reality

Catholicism in New Orleans is inseparable from the cultural and linguistic mosaic that is the pattern of daily life. There are paradoxes and speech patterns that are uniquely identified with the city. They give the y'at a view of the world in which inconsistencies and ideas that would otherwise be mutually exclusive are resolved by intuition and reflex. Experiencing reality in New Orleans is sometimes like an exercise in theology; both involve a degree of mysticism and faith.

To understand the perception of reality that is the birthright of New Orleanians, perform the following exercise. Early in the morning, as the sun is rising, stand at the foot of Canal Street and look from the east bank across the Mississippi River to Algiers Point on the West Bank. As you squint against the sun in your eyes, you realize that New Orleans must be the only place in the world where the sun rises over the west bank of the river because the West Bank is east of the east bank.

To say that New Orleans is different from the rest of the country is a significant understatement. New Orleanians who travel regularly to other parts of the country have learned to adjust to the culture shock and understand that they may not be able to eat red beans and rice for lunch on Monday in Cincinnati and that there are no neutral grounds dividing streets in Cleveland. They adjust to getting directions in terms of north, south, east, and west rather than uptown, downtown, toward the lake, and toward the river. Yet even those New Orleanians who rarely journey west past Kenner or east of Slidell seem to know inherently that theirs is a special place. Despite chronically depressing reports of the health of the city's economy, many Crescent City natives refuse to leave home merely for better jobs. There is too much here, intangible and transcendent, that cannot be transported to Ohio, Missouri, or Oregon.

One of the characteristics least likely to survive a move is a New Orleanian's perception of daily life, the view of "How Things Really Are." There are, in this special niche of the world, unique ways of looking at events, sights, and sounds. The paradox of y'at reality is illustrated by the following true story, an event that took place several years ago after Sunday morning Mass at St. Agnes Church on Jefferson Highway. Across from the church was a small neighborhood bakery that did a brisk business after each Sunday Mass. An elderly lady was poking through the stack of fresh French bread loaves until she found one wrapped in paper showing that it had been baked at Falkenstein's, a local bakery that supplied French bread to retail bakeries. "This is the authentic French bread," she announced with serious emphasis and a vigorous nod. "Mr. Falkenstein brought the recipe with him from Germany." The lady, the neighborhood bakery, and Falkenstein's bread are all long gone, but New Orleanians' view of "authenticity" remains the same.

Sirens

In almost everywhere else in the world, a siren is a scream of anxiety or pain or even terror. It is the signature sound of police cars, fire trucks, or ambulances. But the sound of a siren on New Orleans streets, especially in February, conjures up excitement, expectation, and an imminent street party. A New Orleans siren means the parade is coming.

Red Lights

Motorists in other parts of the world refer to these devices as traffic lights. The reason the New Orleans red light is so called is unknown. Perhaps it is because the only function of a traffic light is to stop traffic, uncontrolled traffic needing no green light to keep it going. Perhaps it is because stopping for a red light adds to the slower pace of a city some call the Big Easy, or perhaps it is because many New Orleans drivers consider the light only a decorative red light, to be noticed in passing but not causing any significant change in the forward movement of their vehicles.

Pass By

Unlike the red light, pass by means that you actually stop, as in, "I'm gonna pass by my Mama's after the Saints game." This means that you will stop and visit, even have a meal, but not spend the night. If you spend the night, especially if you do it regularly, you may be progressing to the condition of "stayin' by your Mama's."

Cemeteries

A graveyard is a somber, sorrowful place for most people.

Deceased family members and friends lie beneath the earth, at rest and in peace, mourned by those who knew and loved them. But the New Orleans departed lie in vaults above the ground where, perhaps, they can better enjoy the sounds of a jazz funeral. Like so much in New Orleans culture, a cemetery is a place of celebration. The flowers and socializing in the cemeteries on All Saints Day may not be unique to New Orleans, but where else can you buy a stick of Roman candy or a couple of pralines from street vendors as you walk away from a visit with the dead? And certainly no cemetery in Minneapolis, Milwaukee, or Missoula has seen second-liners dancing as the band "cuts him loose" and struts away from the tomb. In New Orleans, even the dead party.

Umbrellas

Rain and threatening clouds may come to mind when umbrellas are mentioned in other parts of the country, but the New Orleans umbrella is a flag signaling celebration. Second-liners rally to an appropriately decorated umbrella as the children of Hamelin did to the Pied Piper. The umbrella is a street version of a painter's canvas upon which the artist creates with color, sequins, tulle, and trinkets.

Poor Boy

Of course, this is not a male child living in poverty. If someone used "poor boy" in a conversation in Indianapolis, the listener would not think of French bread. But what would he think if told that, not only does it mean French bread, but it can also mean "lotsa fried ersters drippin' wit' my-nez"? (Translation: "Lots of fried oysters dripping with mayonnaise.")

Desire

This is the dark side of New Orleans' reality. The general meaning of the word "desire" has pleasant connotations of enjoyable yearnings or sexual attraction, but the Desire neighborhood of New Orleans is a place of deep poverty, violent crime, and social gloom. Say the word "desire" to a New Orleanian, and thoughts of fear, desolation, and despair may come to mind.

Fat

Obesity is accepted in New Orleans, somewhat cheerfully, as nothing more than an occupational hazard of eating local food. The word "fat" may sound ugly to a non-New Orleanian, but such names as Fat City, Fat Tuesday, Fat Harry's Bar, and the great monarch of New Orleans rhythm and blues, Fats Domino, proclaim fat as a condition worthy of emulation.

The Flying Horses

This is the quintessence of the New Orleans idiom and its perspective on reality. Elsewhere "carousel" is the term used, but that word is no more than a generic name for a mechanical device that goes around in a circle. For several generations, the carousel in New Orleans City Park has been known to all who care by this name, which signifies fantasy and magic and appropriate images in harmony with the city's spirit of exhilaration and celebration. Ride the Flying Horses one evening as dusk matures into twilight and enter into the heart and soul of a kaleidoscope of sight, sound, and color. The Flying Horses are not just a carousel; they are magic.

The alluvial mud on which New Orleans is built is soil that has been washed away from the heart of the continent. Dreams and fantasies that have been washed away from other hearts and places also come to rest here and thrive, propagate, and mutate. There are streets named Treasure and Pleasure, Duels and Pirates, Hope and Abundance. The main street of the city is named for a canal that was never dug. The architecture of the French Quarter is Spanish-influenced. Spanish Fort at the mouth of Bayou St. John was originally erected by the French. The Crescent City has been home to The Church of the Free Mind and the Church of St. Expedite.

It is no wonder that Catholicism thrives in this culture of paradox and disdain for rational thinking. Belief that a wafer of bread becomes the physical body of Jesus Christ is easier when your daily surroundings and experiences do not require that truth be exclusively based on empirical data. Life and death, redemption and resurrection are not just articles of faith, but realities of daily life in a city that thrives on fantasy and mystery.

CHAPTER 3

Geography

The City of New Orleans was founded by Bienville in 1718. The founder, a French Canadian, was a member of the minor nobility of prerevolutionary France. His Christian name, as it was once called, was Jean-Baptiste Le Moyne, with the added title of Sieur de Bienville. It is ironic that his title name, Bienville, translates into English as "Nicetown." The site he chose for what would become by 1850 one of the largest and richest cities in North America was anything but a nice place to live. It was a swampy forest with the expected residents—snakes, alligators, and mosquitoes. One of the reasons he chose the site is because the native Indians showed him a route from the great waterway that would become known as the Mississippi River to the brackish body of water that would be named Lake Pontchartrain. The most important element in this link between river and lake was a bayou that emptied into the lake and whose far end was a short distance from the river. A portage on relatively high land provided access to the lake from the natural levee of the river.

In the days of sailing ships, one hundred years before steamboats, the trip up the Mississippi River from the Gulf of Mexico to New Orleans, especially if the river was high and the current strong, could take almost as long as the voyage from France to the mouth of the river. Because Lake Pontchartrain was open to the Gulf of Mexico through the Mississippi Sound and the Rigolets and Chef Menteur passes, a voyage to the city could take considerably less time by approaching through Lake Pontchartrain and then into the bayou that cut several miles south to the river. To this vital waterway, a geographic *raison d'être* of the City of New Orleans, Bienville gave the name of his personal patron saint, St. Jean-Baptiste or Bayou St. John.

It is not known whether Bienville was a devout Catholic, although being a French Canadian nobleman prior to the French Revolution did not give him much choice in religious affiliation. The Bourbon kings tended to be partial to members of their Roman faith; believers of other persuasions were shoved aside or worse. Bienville observed the custom of French explorers of the New World by giving religious names to places, a common practice in France before the revolution. But Bienville's choice of his patron saint for the most important geographic feature of the new city, the bayou connecting river and lake, set a tone for the identification of New Orleans with all things Catholic.

St. John the Baptist is described in the New Testament as the precursor of Jesus. He was a fiery prophet who lost his head because his message annoyed King Herod's wife. In one emotional scene in the gospels, John baptized Jesus in the River Jordan, protesting that he was unworthy to do so. Jesus later preached that to be saved you needed to be baptized in the water and the spirit. The sacrament of Baptism originates in these scenes from scripture, and baptism for a Christian is a mark of a new beginning into life with Jesus. Did Bienville also have in mind that the naming of the bayou for St. John the Baptist was the sign of a new beginning?

The bayou's French name disappeared as English began to dominate maritime trade and commerce. The waterway has kept the name of Bayou St. John, although its mouth at Lake Pontchartrain has been closed to navigation for many years.

Giving saints' names to geographic locations was very popular in colonial New Orleans. As John Chase explains in his book, *Frenchmen, Desire, Goodchildren and Other New Orleans Street Names,* saints' names were sometimes given to a street as gratitude to a wealthy benefactor. St. Charles Avenue, for example, was named for the patron saint of King Carlos of Spain. Using saints' names as place names was so popular that early land developers often named streets and neighborhoods after themselves or their associates and simply added "St." in front of their names, whether there was a saint by that name or not. In eastern New Orleans, Lake St. Catherine was named by Bienville for Catherine Knollys, the wife of John Law, his friend and financial benefactor.

The Catholicism of the French and Spanish colonial settlers and administrators was a part of their national identities. Bienville, the first governor of Louisiana, passed a law that prohibited any religion other than Catholicism. The law required that all children, including those of slaves, be baptized into the faith of their king. The Bourbon kings believed, and expected their subjects to do so as well, that their authority to rule was granted through divine right. This sense of authority given by a deity was a far cry from what the Anglo-American free thinkers who created the United States Constitution had in mind when they wrote into the First Amendment that Congress should make no law establishing a state religion. Louisiana royalists would have considered such ideas heresy. Someone who believes that church and state are—or should be—one entity is called in French an *integriste*. In many ways, New Orleanians have never ceased being *integristes* in practice, because the point where religion ceases and secularity begins is not only blurred, but in many ways is irrelevant to life in the Crescent City.

The visual image of a great city is usually an architectural masterpiece. Paris is the Eiffel Tower, London the tower bridge. Philadelphia is Independence Hall and the Liberty Bell. Even American cities named for Catholic saints have visual images of secular architecture. The Golden Gate Bridge is the symbol of San Francisco, and St. Louis's image is a huge arch. On the other hand, some cities are forever linked to religion. Rome is Catholicism, Mecca is Islam. The image of the Eternal City is the Basilica of St. Peter. In Mohammed's most holy city, the image is the black rock of the Kaaba, around which the faithful march seven times.

To an outsider, the mental image of New Orleans is not immediately religious. Quite the contrary, it was traditionally considered by visitors to be a place of sin, in the Protestant sense of sensual pleasures, free-flowing liquor, the fleshpots of Bourbon Street, and the legalized prostitution of Storyville from 1897 to 1917. But the postcard makers and other commercial photographers of the twentieth century saw that St. Louis Cathedral, as seen from the Decatur Street side of Jackson Square, was a better image of the city. From that vantage point, the cathedral presents an aesthetic picture in the symmetry of its spires framed by the Presbytère to its right and the Cabildo to its left. Brochures extolling the attractions of New Orleans as a destination for tourists and conventioneers always include a picture of the cathedral. St. Louis Cathedral is New Orleans.

The cathedral's location, nevertheless, creates a paradox because of the name of the passageway next to it. Is there religious or political significance in the fact that the narrow street between the cathedral and the Cabildo, originally the headquarters of the Spanish colonial government in Louisiana, is Pirate Alley? In New Orleans the physical separation of church and state is a narrow walkway named for criminals.

The cathedral is not merely a tourist attraction. Like St. Peter's in Rome and the cathedral of Notre Dame in Paris, St. Louis Cathedral is a local church where the bishop celebrates Sunday Mass. Parents bring their children there to be baptized, and throngs gather there for Christmas caroling and midnight Mass. While tourists wander about the church and mimes, musicians, and fortunetellers ply their trades out front, prayers are said inside as they are in Catholic churches elsewhere. Local Catholics kneel and pray in the cathedral for such important favors from the Almighty as no rain on Mardi Gras and victory for the hometown Saints football team.

The Catholicism of New Orleans is not just evident in place names and churches. It sometimes leaps up from the ground. As you walk along the streets of the city, looking down at the sidewalk can occasionally be a religious experience. Some of the street names—like St. Ann Street or Grand Route St. John—are displayed in blue and white tiles at the corners and may be read while taking a stroll. Some older sidewalks are of herring-bone or cross-hatched-patterned red brick, and every now and then you come across a brick in the walk that reads "St. Joe." This designation is not a sign that there is a relic of St. Joseph in the brick, but it is a mark of the maker, the St. Joe Brick Works in St. Tammany Parish, on the north shore of Lake Pontchartrain.

Even obscure saints are remembered in New Orleans street names.

St. Joe not only has a brick works named for him. There is a St. Joe's Bar on Magazine Street, where you can buy a T-shirt with a picture of the Holy Family—Jesus, Mary, and St. Joe—all with halos shining brightly.

St. Tammany needs an explanation here. There is no church dedicated to any saint by that name, and the man identified as Tammany was not a Christian. "Tammany" is a corruption of Tammanend, the name of a revered chief of the Delaware Indians of the eighteenth century. He became legendary among the Anglo-Americans in the eastern United States for his decency, honesty, and dignity. Fraternal and political societies were named for him, Tammany Hall of New York City being the best known.

Louisiana's first American governor was a young Virginian, William C. C. Claiborne, who knew about Chief Tammanend or Tammany. Claiborne was not a Catholic, but he married a New Orleans woman who was, and he learned quickly the importance of Catholicism to New Orleanians. When Louisiana was admitted to the union as a state in 1812, Governor Claiborne designated the north shore of Lake Pontchartrain, which was not included in the Louisiana Purchase, St. Tammany Parish. Claiborne's choice of Tammany reflected the many villages of Choctaw people who lived there.

The term "parish," when used by Catholics elsewhere in America, has but one meaning: a church parish. It has both a geographical element, the boundaries of the parish, and an ecclesiastical element, the church building and the people who are members of that parish. In y'at Catholicism, "parish" has many meanings. In addition to a church parish, "parish" in Louisiana is a term designating a division of the state, the same as "county" in the other forty-nine states. Depending on usage in New Orleans speech, "the Parish" can mean St Bernard civil parish, the next parish downriver from New Orleans on the east bank of the Mississippi River, which is pronounced *SAIN-buh-NAWD,* not *SAINT-BER-nid,* as the nuns tried to teach children in elementary school. Many y'ats migrated to St. Bernard Parish in the 1950s and 1960s. To them their home is *the* parish. The New Orleans jail is officially called the Orleans Parish Prison, but in colloquial speech and courthouse slang, it is sometimes referred to as "the Parish." To complicate matters even more, there is a music club in the French Quarter called the Parish. These many meanings and usages of "parish" could result in the following hypothetical conversation between two y'ats:

"Where you living these days?"

"I stay by my mama's, by Nashville and Laurel."

"Oh, yeah. That's St. Francis Parish."

"Yeah. Last night I was listening to Dr. John; he was playing at the Parish. I went with A. J. and them."

"Aren't they from the Parish?"

"Yeah, A. J.'s daddy just got out after spending six months in the Parish."

Every y'at would understand that conversation and what meaning to assign to each use of "parish." St. Francis of Assisi Parish is on State Street near Nashville Avenue and Laurel Street. The Parish music club is on Decatur Street. A. J.'s father was just let out of the Orleans Parish Prison, and A. J. is from St. Bernard Parish. Very simple.

Contrary to popular myth, the designation of the political subdivisions of Louisiana as parishes rather than counties has nothing to do with the Napoleonic Code. Despite what Tennessee Williams wrote for Stanley Kowalski to speak in *A Streetcar Named Desire,* the Napoleonic Code was never in force in Louisiana. The Code Napoleon and the Code Civil Francais were used to formulate the Louisiana Civil Code, but none of those legal documents designates the civil divisions of the state as parishes rather than counties. That practice seems to have been another result of Louisiana's lack of interest in the separation of church and state. The church had its parishes in place geographically when the American civil authorities got around to drawing the lines and naming the subdivisions. It was easier to adopt the existing ecclesiastical boundaries than to draw new ones. As a result there are civil parishes in Louisiana named St. James, St. John the Baptist, Ascension,

Assumption, St. Mary, St. Landry, St. Helena, St. Bernard, and St. Martin, among others. There would be much irony in the possible scene of an attorney representing the American Civil Liberties Union arguing a lawsuit challenging state-supported religious services in a courthouse named for a Catholic saint. Perhaps that lawyer would be thinking or muttering or praying as she or he ascends the court-house steps, "Thank God I'm an atheist."

In addition to streets named for saints, New Orleans has streets named for nuns, Nuns Street, to be exact. There are also Religious Street and Ursulines Street, the latter named for the order of French nuns who established the first school and convent in New Orleans. The apparent piety of the original city planners is also evidenced by Piety Street. But what is most significant about Piety Street is that it intersects with Abundance, Treasure, and Pleasure streets. It is also parallel to and separated by one short block from Desire Street. It was the streetcar that ran down the middle of Desire Street that inspired the name of Tennessee Williams's famous play. Would the play have been such a success had he named it for the streetcar that ran on Piety Street? There is something very significant about the fact that Piety and Desire are very close to each other, but never intersect or touch. Is there another place in the world where two people can agree to meet at the corner of Piety and Pleasure, one block from Desire?

CHAPTER 4

Churches

Like other dioceses in America, the Archdiocese of New Orleans consists of many church parishes located throughout the city and in several adjacent civil parishes. These churches are dedicated, just as elsewhere, to various saints; Mary, under many different titles; and other names of spiritual and theological significance. There was even one church whose official name is in Spanish, San Pedro Pescador or St. Peter the Fisherman, in St. Bernard Parish. That church was given a Spanish name because the congregation was composed of the descendants of the Isleños, the fisher families of the Canary Islands who settled there during the Spanish colonial period. The church was closed indefinitely after Hurricane Katrina flooded it in 2005. Despite the strong French influence in New Orleans, there are no churches with French names. The seminary of the archdiocese has a French name, Notre Dame, and the spelling of St. Louis Cathedral is the same in English and in French, but no churches have French names, not even St. Joan of Arc in the Carrollton neighborhood. The bishops who approved the names felt comfortable with Latin, and there are churches named Mater Dolorosa (Sorrowful Mother) and Corpus Christi (Body of Christ), but no French.

There are churches in New Orleans whose official names are different from the names used by the y'at faithful to identify their churches. For example, if a New Orleanian told a tourist to attend Mass at Holy Rosary Church on a Jazz Fest Sunday because of its proximity to the Fair Grounds, where the festival is held, the visitor would not be able to locate that church in the phone book. Every y'at in New Orleans knows that Holy Rosary is the beautiful, old church with the dome on Esplanade Avenue near City Park. Most people probably do not know, or have any reason to care, that the real name of Holy Rosary Church is Our Lady of the Rosary. Like so much else in the culture of New Orleans, there is a murky gap between the perception of reality and reality itself.

In the Gentilly neighborhood, between the French Quarter and Lake Pontchartrain, there is a church named for St. James. Unlike the Anglican-Episcopalians or the Spanish, the bishops who named American Catholic churches designated between the two Jameses who were apostles. One is known as James the Less to differentiate him from the other James, who is known as James the Great or James Major. The English refer to the Royal British Court as the Court of St. James, and in Spain, the most famous shrine and place of pilgrimage is Campostella, a site at which the relics of St. James ("Santiago" in Spanish) are believed to rest. Both the English and the Spanish seem to take for granted that St. James/Santiago is the apostle named in the scriptures as the son of Zebedee and brother of St. John.

All this biblical information is not important to y'at Catholics. They know that the church in Gentilly is St. James Major, but they often call it St. James the Major (pronounced *DA MAY-juh*), inviting an inference that St.

James was some sort of army officer. There is no church in New Orleans dedicated to St. James the Less.

The use of the term "St. James the Major" reveals an interesting linguistic pattern in the New Orleans vernacular. Y'ats like to put the article "the" in front of names. It may be a vestigial holdover from French, which uses articles much more than English. For example, the articles "le" and "la" appear at the front of many French names. LeBlanc, Lesage, Laplace, and LeBoeuf are frequently seen examples. Y'ats also use articles in nicknames. A well-known New Orleans character, the late Louis Nugent, a geologist-turned-firefighter and raconteur, is known as "The Nuge," more accurately pronounced *DA-nooge*. A dynamic mayor of the city in the 1970s ran for office under his given name, Maurice Landrieu. After winning the mayor's office, he officially changed his identity to his nickname, Moon. Mayor Moon Landrieu was then called "the Moon" by y'ats. In adjacent Jefferson Parish, because of the obvious connection with his last name, Deputy Constable Larry Pontiff is known as "The Pope." Even his family members call him that, and he uses the title in the telephone directory.

Charity Hospital, the largest and oldest in the city, is often called "the Charity" or, even more frequently, "the Big Charity." Several years ago, state officials officially changed its name to the Medical Center of Louisiana at New Orleans, but nobody noticed. It remains in popular usage as "the Big Charity." The hospital once known as Hotel Dieu, named for the ancient Paris hospital founded by St. Landry, was called "the Hotel Dieu," but its recent name change to University Hospital seems to have stuck.

The hospital named in the old jazz dirge "St. James Infirmary" doesn't exist and may never have. The mournful lyrics of the song do not specify to which St. James the hospital was dedicated. Somehow "St. James Major Infirmary" doesn't sound right. Just to confuse everybody even more, there is a small hotel in the Central Business District called the St. James Hotel that has no connection to St. James Major Church or, one would hope, St. James Infirmary. There is, however, a St. James Hospital in Lutcher, Louisiana, in St. James civil parish. It is a psychiatric facility.

Despite the absent article in St. James's church name, there are, nevertheless, churches in New Orleans dedicated to saints with "the" in their titles: St. Leo the Great, who was a pope; St. Edward the Confessor, who was king of England; St. Gabriel the Archangel, who blows his horn; and St. Matthew the Apostle, tax man and patron saint of the IRS. All of them have churches dedicated to them in the archdiocese. So why did St. James get "the" left out of his name, only to be reinserted by the worshipful y'ats? It may be one of those theological mysteries that are taught in parochial school, incapable of comprehension by humans.

St. Christopher the Martyr Church in Metairie had the qualification "the martyr" added to its name in the 1960s, long after the church had been built and dedicated to the better-known plain St. Christopher. The original St. Christopher, whose name is derived from the Greek word for "Christ carrier," is the saint whose medals and miniature statues were once a necessity in automobiles. Christopher was the patron saint of travelers based on the legend that he was a huge man who worked as a ferryman, carrying people across a raging stream. One day, so the story goes, he was carrying a child who became heavier and heavier as Big Chris forded the stream. Bowed by the weight of the child, the ferryman asked to set him down. The child then identified himself as Jesus and told Christopher that he was carrying the weight of the sins of the world. Christopher then became a true believer and began preaching Christianity throughout the land. It's a good story, but in the hagiological reforms of the 1960s, the Vatican gave the legendary ferryman the theological ax and declared that he was never a real person, just a legend. St. Christopher's Church in Metairie could not, under canon law, be named for a fake saint, so an obscure but real martyr, also named St. Christopher, was selected, and the church was rededicated to him. Most y'ats neither know nor care that the Christopher of St. Christopher's Church is not the patron of travelers. Many call the church St. Christopher's in Metairie, which makes it sound like some place that English gentlemen ride to the hounds in red coats and white pants.

Y'ats do not like to change long-accepted names of places and churches. The main street of New Orleans, Canal Street, was named for a canal that was never dug. In the 1850s, the name was changed to Touro Street, after financier Judah Touro. No one called it Touro Street, and it was officially changed back to Canal Street a few years later. Many older New Orleanians still call the Fairmont Hotel the Roosevelt, even though it lost that identity more than a generation ago. In 1964, officials in the Vatican decided to upgrade the status of St. Louis Cathedral. It was made a minor basilica under church rules that are concerned with such matters. The Cathedral, as it is known to all y'at Catholics, was officially changed to the Basilica of St Louis. Most y'at Catholics did not know what a basilica was, but it sounded like something served in a Greek restaurant that has a tape playing bouzouki music. Nobody but the people who worked in the Chancery Office of the Archdiocese and dealt with the people in the Vatican referred to the Cathedral as the Basilica. The new name quietly went away, and everybody returned to calling the Cathedral its correct y'at name.

In the heart of the business district, in the first block off Canal Street, is a church known to y'ats as Jesuits' Church (pronounced *JEZ-wit*). It is located right across the street from the fondly remembered, if incorrectly labeled, Roosevelt Hotel. Its official name is Immaculate Conception Parish, but that name shows up only on the church bulletin and other official documents. Even the listings in the telephone directory show the name Jesuit Church rather than Church of the Immaculate Conception. Y'at Catholics identify this church with the priests who run it rather than the somewhat mystical and theologically arcane doctrine of the Immaculate Conception, which holds that Mary, the mother of Jesus, was conceived without original sin, unlike the rest of humanity, and hence her soul is spotless, or immaculate.

The Jesuits of the Jesuit Church have a long and colorful history in New Orleans. Very early in the French settlement of Louisiana, the Society of Jesus, the official name of the order, acquired a large plantation that included the site where their church now sits. In the 1750s, a dispute in Europe between the superior of the Jesuits and the superior of the Capuchins, another religious order, became very political, resulting in the French government expelling the Jesuits from all French colonies in 1763. The Pope went along with the suppression, and the Jesuits were expelled from New Orleans and their lands confiscated, despite the fact that before the date of the decree in 1764, Louisiana and New Orleans had secretly been transferred from France to Spain in the 1762 Treaty of Fontainebleau. Years later the wily Jesuits made their way back to New Orleans and reestablished themselves as dominant players in the city's religious, social, and educational life. The Jesuits also are assigned to the only Catholic church on St. Charles Avenue. The Black Robes, as they were once called by the North American Indians who assassinated several of their brethren in the eighteenth century, run Loyola University, which fronts on St. Charles Avenue and part of which is a large and beautiful church. The official name of this church is the Most Holy Name of Jesus, but hardly anyone, not even the pastor, calls it that anymore, if they ever did. If a y'at hears someone speak of Holy Name, he immediately knows that it is the church on St. Charles. There is another Holy Name church in New Orleans, Holy Name of Mary in Algiers. It is never referred to as Holy Name, and the full name is always used by y'at Catholics so as not to confuse the two. Why the church named for Jesus got a "most" in front of its name is an unanswered question. The namers must have had a tendency to unnecessary, needless, superfluous redundancies.

In Algiers, there is a church dedicated to St. Andrew the Apostle. He is one of the saints who gets a "the" and a title. Maybe adding the title is to prevent confusion with an Episcopal church in the Carrollton neighborhood named St. Andrew's. St. Andrew is not only an apostle, but he is also the patron saint of Scotland and golf. The faithful congregation of the Carrollton St. Andrew's would hardly be expected to call their church St. Andrew the Episcopalian or St. Andrew the Golfer, so it is simply St. Andrew's. St. Andrew's Episcopal Church runs a highly respected grade school that for many years had a Catholic headmaster with a Jewish name, Mr. Rosenberg. This is New Orleans; it should not be a surprise.

There are many churches in New Orleans named for St. Francis. Because there are many saints by that name, it is important to keep them separate. Uptown is St. Francis of Assisi; in Metairie there is St. Francis Xavier. The Gospel choir of St. Francis de Sales in Central City is properly famous for its raise-the-roof, high-energy spirituals. In Gentilly, a big church was dedicated to St. Frances Xavier Cabrini, but it was known by y'at Catholics simply as Cabrini. The archdiocese closed it after Katrina.

One of the newest saints, who served the faithful in nineteenth-century New Orleans until he was felled by yellow fever, is Blessed Francis Xavier Seelos, a German Redemptorist priest. Even though he is not yet fully canonized, he will undoubtedly continue to be known and venerated in New Orleans as Father Seelos. Another St. Francis is unnecessary. Father Seelos even has a parish dedicated to him, situated in the old St. Vincent de Paul Church on Dauphine Street. Father Seelos's parish was created out of five old church parishes in the neighborhood whose membership and attendance had declined due to changing demographics and economics. The archdiocese combined the closed Annunciation, St. Vincent's, St. Cecilia's, St. Gerard's, and Sts. Peter and Paul to form the new parish.

The vigor and vibrancy of New Orleans Catholicism are well manifested in this parish named for a hometown saint. The new parish is active with many ministries, including serving the deaf and the Spanish-speaking residents of the neighborhood. The resurrection of an old, closed church in a decaying neighborhood is a miracle in itself, one that should be used to convince the Vatican that Father Francis Xavier Seelos is entitled to full sainthood.

One of the most popular devotions among y'at Catholics

and even some y'ats who aren't completely Catholic is the novena to St. Jude. It is conducted four times a year in the church of Our Lady of Guadalupe. Lots of people are either unaware or uninterested in the fact that the official name of the church is not St. Jude's. The devotion to the saint is the most popular event that takes place in that church, and it is usually called the St. Jude Shrine, after its adjacent garden dedicated to the saint. St. Jude, one of the twelve apostles, is venerated as the patron saint of hopeless cases or patron saint of the impossible. This is tough theological work, to say the least. The story about how St. Jude got such hard duty is that he is one of the most obscure of the apostles, with little actually known of his

Is there a connection between the large sign urging prayer to St. Jude below the small sign advertising a casino?

life and mission. Unlike most of the other apostles, whose intercession was invoked for various causes or places, Jude had no such identity. In the Middle Ages he was avoided because his name was too much like Judas, and the praying faithful did not want their prayers going to someone they thought was surely in hell. St. Jude, therefore, became the saint to whom the desperate prayed when they needed last-ditch help.

St. Jude's geographical location in New Orleans is very telling. The church is on North Rampart Street, facing the French Quarter. The rear of the church is on Basin Street, across from St. Louis Cemetery. Immediately adjacent to the cemetery is the area that was once Storyville, a place of legalized prostitution from 1897 to 1917. Also, the original church on the site of Our Lady of Guadalupe was the Old Mortuary Chapel, given that name because of its proximity to the graveyard. It was built to provide a place for services for the many victims of yellow fever in the nineteenth century. In such a location with so much sordid history nearby, the saint of the impossible has his work cut out for him.

The double dedication of the church and the shrine is because in the early 1920s New Orleans anticipated an influx of Mexican immigrants, and the archdiocese wanted to have a church ready for them in which they would feel welcome. The Mexicans stayed south of the border for the most part, but the name remained on the church.

The church building of Our Lady of Guadalupe is relatively small, but it houses a great variety of statues. Inside are images of St. Martha, St. Martin de Porres, St. Joseph, St. Dymphna, St. Florian, St. Michael the Archangel, St. Ann, St. Raymond, and St. Anthony of Padua. Y'at Catholics like to cover all their bases when they ask for favors from the Lord, so maybe having this big array of holy helpers helps get divine attention more quickly. There is also a statue in the church to St. Expedite, whose tale is a New Orleans legend. No one knows who St. Expedite is or was or if he even existed at all. The legend is that a crate arrived at a convent in Paris from Italy containing the body of a saint from the catacombs. There was no name on the box, but the word "Expedito" was stenciled on the wood of the crate. That was good enough for the believers, and the cult of St. Expedite took off from there. Unfortunately, there is no Catholic church in New Orleans dedicated to this mysterious holy man. There are "holy pictures" of St. Expedite available for sale at the St. Jude Shrine and other locations. "Holy pictures" are cards, usually printed in Europe, with highly stylized paintings of saints that are used in devotions and as bookmarks in prayer books. The holy picture of St. Expedite shows a very young, baby-faced Roman soldier holding high in his right hand a cross on which the Latin word *hodie* is emblazoned. Under his foot is a hideous bird above whose beak is a cartoon-style balloon with the word *cras*. *Hodie* means today, and *cras* translates to tomorrow. A prayer to St. Expedite is protection from procrastination. The prayer to him printed on the back of the holy picture asks the Lord, through the help of St. Expedite, for "courage, fidelity, and promptitude, at the time proper and favorable." At one time there was a St. Expedite Spiritualist Church, a sect that incorporates Catholic, Protestant, and West African traditions, but the church closed several years ago.

The National Shrine of St. Jude is the repository of what is described in the information brochure as the world's largest statue of St. Jude. This cannot be an exaggeration. When you gaze on the imposing, intimidating, almost ominous bronze

St. Jude, patron saint of hopeless cases, is a favorite among y'ats. This statue in the courtyard of Our Lady of Guadalupe Church stands seventeen feet from his bronze soles to the tip of his Pentecostal tongue of fire (club included).

effigy rising seventeen feet from its pedestal to the tip of its Pentecostal tongue of flame at the top of the saint's head, it is absurd to consider that anyone would even consider making a statue of the saint of impossible causes that is bigger. The image is so dark and huge that it is almost threatening. Jude holds in his right hand, typical of artistic depiction of martyr saints, the instrument of his martyrdom, a huge club. It looks like something you might see in a comic strip about cave men. The statue is too large to be inside the church, so it is in an open area outside the church that has been curiously designated the Peace Garden. This may be to remind believers that should they, like Jude, get whacked with one of those clubs, they too will experience everlasting peace.

The term "shrine" in the Catholic tradition refers to a place, not necessarily a church, that is so designated to encourage a certain devotion. New Orleans frequently has conventions of shriners, and the Shrine Circus has been an annual event in the city since the 1950s. Shriners are the men wearing decorated fezzes who sometimes ride motorcycles and dune buggies in carnival parades. However, the shriners are part of the Masonic Lodge movement, and they have nothing to do with Catholicism. They raise a lot of money for charitable operations, such as a hospital for burn victims.

The Catholic shrines of New Orleans include the National Shrines to St. Ann, Our Lady of Prompt Succor, St. Roch, and St. Lazarus of Jerusalem, which are discussed in a subsequent chapter. There are uncounted personal shrines throughout the city, the most common of which are yard shrines to the Blessed Mother. Some of these use half of an old oval-shaped tub, set up vertically to form a grotto to house a statue of the Virgin. Other yard shrines popular with y'ats are to St. Francis of Assisi and St. Joseph. St. Francis shrines often include a bird bath or bird feeder. St. Francis is said to have preached to the birds and wild animals when people would not pay attention to him. Y'ats generally think that yard shrines to St. Francis, St. Joseph, and the Blessed Mother have more class than shiny yard balls and fake flamingoes. Besides, the St. Francis bird feeders are a good place to get rid of stale bread.

Despite all the streets named for saints, the only active church in the city of New Orleans located on a street of the same name is St. Maurice, in the lower Ninth Ward. St. Maurice was a Roman soldier and martyr, and his church is on St. Maurice Street. There is a church dedicated to St. Ann, but it is not on St. Ann Street. Neither is St. Phillip's Church on St. Phillip Street, and so forth. Across the Mississippi River in Marrero, the Catholic Vietnamese immigrants dedicated a church to St. Lê Thi Thành. Agnes Lê Thi Thành was one of many Catholic martyrs in nineteenth-century Vietnam. Local officials accommodated the parishioners and renamed the street alongside the church St. Le Thi Thanh Street, but the sign shop of the Streets Department was not equipped to make street signs with accent marks. So the parishioners located a very precise sign painter, and the sign on the fence around the church property informs that it is St. Lê Thi Thành Church, 6851 Saint Le Thi Thanh St. No matter; the saint is honored even without the marks. However, the church is listed in the archdiocesan directory as being on Westwood Drive, which is two streets away.

St. Rita is the patroness of battered women. In Cascia, Italy, in the fifteenth century, Rita was married to a violent drunk and philanderer who abused her physically and emotionally. After he was murdered (not by her), Rita's sons vowed vengeance and sought to kill their father's murderer. Rita could not abide the idea of her sons becoming murderers, too, so she prayed to God that they might be taken up to heaven before they committed the heinous deed. God apparently heard her prayers, and the angry sons were struck with a fatal disease, which presumably sent them to heaven, as Mama Rita wanted. This shows that sainthood is available even to those who wish their children dead, but only for the right reason.

But why in the Archdiocese of New Orleans are there two churches dedicated to St. Rita? Is New Orleans so full of wife beaters and mothers that pray for their children to be dead that the good women of the city need two churches where they can invoke her protection and intercession? The archdiocese does run battered-women's shelters, but they are not in either of the St. Rita parishes. To distinguish the two St. Rita churches, y'ats usually refer to St. Rita on Lowerline or St. Rita in Carrollton and St. Rita in Harahan, giving the holy woman new titles not thought of by the institutional church.

The largest church in the archdiocese of New Orleans is the huge, magnificent St. Joseph's on Tulane Avenue. But this gigantic church is not enough devotion to St. Joseph for y'at Catholics, because across the Mississippi River are three churches dedicated to the patron saint of the universal church. St. Joseph has a church dedicated to him in Algiers, considerably smaller than the grand building on Tulane Avenue, and in Marrero, there is the church of St. Joseph the Worker. Marrero and much of the rest of the west bank of the Mississippi River are blue-collar suburbia, with shipyards, oil-field support industries, and railroad yards, making St. Joseph as patron saint of working people appropriate for that area. The title of St. Joseph as the worker came about as a counter to communist influence in the labor movement. The Vatican, under the direction of Pope Pius XII, picked May 1, May Day, the biggest day in the international communist movement, as the feast day of St. Joseph the Worker, although they decided against adopting the red hammer-and-sickle flag as his emblem. This day is in addition to St. Joseph's main feast day, March 19. There is a St. Joseph Street in the Warehouse District of New Orleans, but there is no church to St. Joseph there.

Gretna is another West Bank community with a church of St. Joseph. The Gretna church does not give him a title, such as the worker. Because Joseph was the husband of Mary, the mother of Jesus, you wonder why there is no church dedicated to St. Joseph the Understanding Husband. After all, it had to be very difficult for him to believe that his pregnant bride-to-be was still a virgin. Another appropriate title for St. Joseph, who is also a patron saint of Italy, could be the Romans' phrase for the head of the family, the *Bonus Paterfamilias*, literally translated as the "Good Father of the Family."

There is only one parish church in the French Quarter, St. Louis Cathedral. There is one other Catholic church, but it is not a parish, and it has had many name changes since it was first established. The Great Fire of 1788 destroyed or seriously damaged almost all of New Orleans, leaving the Ursuline Convent the only untouched structure. That building is no longer used as a convent and school, but serves as the repose of the archives of the archdiocese. Next to the Ursuline Convent is a small church that is now designated, in brass letters attached to the front wall facing Chartres Street, St. Mary's Church. A plaque on the wall informs passers-by that the church was originally called the Archbishops' Chapel. It was dedicated to Our Lady of Victory when it was built in 1846 and was used by the archbishops for daily Mass. With the influx of Italian immigrants into the French Quarter in the late 1890s, it became the parish church of those new arrivals. In 1920, the name was officially changed to St. Mary's Italian Church, and it became a separate parish in 1924. Several generations of Italian-Americans called the small church their parish. As they began to dominate the social and commercial life of the French Quarter, the Italian-Americans of St. Mary's Italian Church acquired an old ice house next to the church at the corner of Chartres and Governor Nicholls streets and constructed a community center in 1948. Its gymnasium was the training ground for many famous and not-so-famous professional boxers. The success of these boxers is another manifestation of the mysteries of Marian theology. By reading the New Testament and the writings of the early fathers of the church, you wouldn't know that Mary is fond of pugilism, but she must have liked to watch the Friday night fights because many of the men who trained at St. Mary's Italian Gymnasium did well as professionals.

By 1970, the Italian-Americans were moving out of the French Quarter, and the archdiocese changed the name of the church back to Our Lady of Victory. But there were too many cultural, emotional, and spiritual connections with the church for the generations of departed Italian-Americans who knew it by its former name. They pressured the archdiocese to return to the name by which they knew the church. Pointing out that it had had another name prior to being St. Mary's Italian, the archdiocese compromised and renamed the little church St. Mary's

Church. It is no longer a separate parish, as it was from 1924 until the 1970s. In an exquisite display of what can be described as "church-speak," the official designation of St. Mary's Church is "a canonical chapel of ease." No one, not even the most committed ecclesiastical bureaucrat, when asked whether he is going to church, would answer, "No, I'm going to a canonical chapel of ease." In a song that was a national hit in the 1960s, three musically talented young New Orleans women, calling themselves "The Dixie Cups," sang and recorded "Goin' to the Chapel," a sweet ballad about getting married. Would it have been a national hit or even recorded at all had it been named "Goin' to the Canonical Chapel of Ease"?

There is no St. Anthony Church on St. Anthony Street. The church dedicated to St. Anthony of Padua (pronounced *SANT-nee*) fronts on Canal Street and is flanked on the right by St. Patrick Street. St. Patrick's Church is nowhere nearby, certainly not on St. Patrick Street. St. Patrick's is in the Arts/Warehouse District on Camp Street, only a block and a half from its intersection with St. Joseph Street, on which is not any of the aforementioned St. Joseph churches. Go figure.

The late Monsignor John Reynolds, a longtime pastor of St. Patrick's, liked to explain that St. Patrick's Church was the first church outside of the Vieux Carré and was thus "the first place in New Orleans that God spoke in English." St. Patrick's has seen its neighborhood change many times. From a commercial and residential part of the Faubourg Ste. Marie, the area deteriorated in the mid-twentieth century into the grimiest part of the city. Flophouses and dirty, dingy barrooms that catered to street people and derelicts surrounded the church. Mass attendees were likely to find empty liquor bottles near the church entrance. In the late 1970s, the gentrification of the neighborhood began at the same time that St. Patrick's launched a major and expensive renovation project. For the next fifteen years, the church and neighborhood slowly were rejuvenated. Today, the neighborhood is known as the Arts District with stylish and trendy art galleries, museums, coffee shops, and restaurants replacing the bars and flop-houses. One of St. Patrick's Church's neighbor's was until very recently a Zen temple, and expensive condominiums and offices are available for those with the money to pay. Original abstract art and hand-crafted blown-glass objets d'art are available to those walking to and from Mass. In the midst of all this trendy modernization and "New Age" spir-ituality, St. Patrick's has remained a guardian of Catholic tradition by offering a Mass in Latin every Sunday morning. *Benedicamus Domino. Deo gratias.*

Not only is the city's cathedral dedicated to St. Louis, but there is a parish church in Bucktown near Lake Pontchartrain called St. Louis King of France. These are named for the same man. He is also the guy for whom the biggest city in Missouri is named. St. Louis is King Louis IX, monarch of France in the thirteenth century. Although he had a disastrous record as a crusader and his vigorous anti-Semitism is reprehensible by today's standards, his deserved fame and holiness are due to his compassion and fairness toward his subjects. He established a three hun-dred-bed hospital for the sick and blind and was famous for his impartiality in administering justice. Most important to Louisiana, he was the patron saint of King Louis XIV (pro-nounced *LOU-ie DA FO-teenth*) for whom Louisiana is named. The early French explorers wanted to make sure that they got King Louis's attention because not only was the territory named for the king and saint, but the original name they gave to Lake Pontchartrain was Lake St. Louis, and the Mississippi was to the first French explorers the St. Louis River. St. Louis Street in the Vieux Carré, is, like other streets with saints' names, several blocks away from St. Louis Cathedral and miles away from Bucktown's church.

Some of the apostles, the personal friends and companions of Jesus, got left out of the church names in New Orleans. Of the thirteen apostles, including St. Matthias who replaced Judas Iscariot after he betrayed Jesus and committed suicide, four are not represented in the archdiocese's churches. One is the previously mentioned St. James the Less, and it is understandable that the name hardly inspires confidence and Christian fortitude. The unfortunate name makes the holy man sound as though he were the runt of the litter or a rejected stepchild like Cinderella. The official church would do well to give him a name change because he is an important person in the New Testament. He was the one whose mother stood at the cross after Jesus was crucified. He, like the other apostles, was probably scared to show his face after the Crucifixion, but he later became the first bishop of Jerusalem and may have been the author of the Epistle of James.

St. Bartholomew does not have a New Orleans church either. The "Bar" in his name identifies him as the son of Tholman, and the scriptures suggest that his first name is Nathaniel. Maybe he was Nathaniel Tholmanson, but there are too many letters in that name to put on the front of a church, and nobody would know who he was. St. Bartholomew is little known to most y'at Catholics, and it is probably just as well that he gets no attention in the Crescent City. He does not even have a street named for him. Maybe the church leaders were uneasy about bringing up the name of St. Bartholomew because on his feast day,

August 24, 1572, a mob of vicious Catholics massacred thousands of Protestants in Paris.

There was another apostle named Simon besides St. Peter, who changed his name after Jesus told him he was the "rock." The other Simon is called by the Gospel writers the Canaanite or the Zealot. Canaanite merely designates where he came from. It would be as if there were a church dedicated to "St. Joe Bob the Texan" or to "St. Boudreaux the Cajun." The title zealot would not look too good on the front of a church building. The term refers to a radical Jewish sect that advocated the violent overthrow of Roman rule. Such a name on a church would be confusing if the Sunday sermon were on Jesus' exhortation to "turn the other cheek" or to "render unto Caesar that which is Caesar's." Do not look for the church of St. Simon the Zealot in New Orleans.

A fourth apostle for whom there is no church in New Orleans is one of the best known, St. John. He is sometimes identified in the New Testament as the youngest apostle, the "one whom Jesus loved," a curious designation implying that Jesus did not love the other eleven. He is sometimes considered the author of the Gospel of John and the writer of the last book of the New Testament, the weird and spooky Book of Revelation. But he has no church in the archdiocese. There are churches dedicated to relatively obscure saints like St. Brigid, St. Julian Eymard, and St. Benilde. Maybe y'ats think St. John was a Protestant, or they shy away because they think his name sounds like a code word for the restroom. St. John the Apostle, the Evangelist, the Revealer has no place to call home in the Crescent City.

The archdiocese should give serious thought to naming a church after St John of the Book of Revelation. That wondrous document's descriptions of fantasies sound as though they were written by someone with a buzz on watching Mardi Gras parades and costumes. Y'ats understand the theology of the Book of Revelation readily. On Mardi Gras, y'ats see lots of angels blowing trumpets and riders on pale horses.

One of the most spirited churches in the Archdiocese of New Orleans is a very old one, St. Augustine in Faubourg Tremé, just outside the Vieux Carré. St. Augustine's Church was founded in 1841 to serve the free black people and Creoles of color. Even though most free blacks and Creoles of color of that period were Catholic, the racial protocols of the day did not permit them to sit in the same pews with white people. They were required to stand or kneel in the back of the church. In response to this, they decided to construct their own church building. When the white people saw this, they started a drive to buy as many pews as they could to prevent the blacks from having their own church. Buying or renting pews in churches was a practice that continued into the twentieth century. The "War of the Pews" at St. Augustine began, and the blacks and Creoles of color who had worked so hard to get a church of their own decided to reserve pews for the enslaved blacks, too. When the church was completed in 1842, it became the first mixed congregation in the city, with free people of color, slaves, and whites sitting in the same church if not in the same pews.

Today St. Augustine's ten o'clock Sunday Mass is a liturgy of spiritual and cultural fusion. Most of the parishioners are black, and the liturgy relies on the rich musical and dramatic heritage of the African-American experience. There are traditional hymns, old Negro spirituals, jazz spirituals, Gospel music, and contemporary hymns. The stained-glass windows are inscribed in French and depict some traditional French saints such as St. Genevieve, patroness of Paris; St. Joan of Arc, the Maid of Orleans; and St. Martin of Tours, the Roman soldier shown giving his cloak to a beggar. There are other very obscure French saints depicted in the windows, too. There is St. Remi, bishop of Reims, who has a brand of very good Champagne named after him, and a St. Radegonde, a German prioress of a convent in Poitiers, France. The old French lettering above the main altar and on the stained-glass windows is contrasted by banners, eight each in English and Swahili, listing the principles of the African-American festival of Kwanzaa. Father Jerome Ledoux, formerly the pastor, returns occasionally to celebrate Mass, which he accomplishes in vestments inspired by West African style of dress. The mood of the congregation is reminiscent of the Gospel tent at the New Orleans Jazz and Heritage Festival.

In the aftermath of Hurricane Katrina, the archdiocese wanted to close St. Augustine because there were too few parishioners. The decision created much opposition and protests because of the historical and cultural importance of the church, especially to blacks and Creoles of color. The decision to close was revoked, and the church was opened provisionally to see if the parish could sufficiently recover financially to continue operating.

On the first weekend in August, usually one of the slowest periods of the year for tourism, the city of New Orleans stages the Satchmo Summerfest, a festival of music, art, and food celebrating the birthday of New Orleans's most famous musician, Louis "Satchmo" Armstrong. Armstrong was baptized in the Catholic Church, specifically at Sacred Heart Church on Canal Street. It is thus appropriate that Satchmo Summerfest be observed with a special Mass, and

St. Augustine is the logical church for such a Mass. For the occasion, the stained-glass windows with stylized pictures of French saints from fifteen hundred years ago are augmented by a large photograph of Armstrong, surely a New Orleans secular saint if there ever was one, at the front of the church close to the band and choir. Ordinarily, Mass is over when the priest or deacon says, "Go in peace to love and to serve the Lord." Not so at the Satchmo Mass. The congregation struts out of the church singing "When the Saints Go Marchin' In" or a comparable high-energy spiritual. On the street in front of the church, a parade forms for a march to Armstrong Park on North Rampart Street and then back to the Old Mint. Mass is a celebration; a parade is a celebration. They go together.

Only two blocks from the Notre Dame Seminary and the Chancery Office of the Archdiocese of New Orleans is a small church on Apricot Street dedicated to the Incarnate Word (pronounced *in-CAWN-nit WOID*). This church provides an opportunity for those priests attached to the Chancery Office with no parish assignment to get pastoral experience and keep in touch with the worshiping faithful. The building that once housed the Incarnate Word Parochial School has become a major administrative and food-collection site for the archdiocese's social-service programs. The name of the church is the result of a somewhat awkward translation of New Testament Greek. The Gospel of John begins, "In the beginning was the Word, and the Word was with God, and the Word was God." In classical Greek the word *logos* was used, and its meaning is much broader than "word" in English. *Logos* is a philosophical concept of the rational principle that governs and develops the universe. Somehow this word got translated into Latin as *verbum,* which is much closer to the English "word." The adjective "incarnate" has the same Latin origin as the "carn" in carnival and the delicious roast beef on menus in Mexican restaurants called carne asada. It means flesh or meat. What "incarnate word" means is that the word, as expressed by St. John, became flesh. The doctrine of the incarnation, Jesus becoming a human being, is expressed sometimes as "the word made flesh." Most y'at Catholics, especially those who went to parochial school, are familiar with the term "word made flesh," but probably wouldn't go to a church with that name.

In fact, the word "word" has many meanings, to y'ats as well as to outsiders. When used by evangelical Protestants, it usually means the Bible, the Holy Scriptures. ("Listen to the Word of God, brothers. . . . ") An evangelical church on Airline Drive in Metairie has a large sign in front displaying its telephone number: 831-WORD. In computer-speak, "Word" is shorthand for the software program Microsoft Word. ("Are you using Word on your PC?") In naval jargon, "the word" is the pertinent latest information or orders. ("The word is that this ship is being sent to the Arabian Sea.") Older y'ats will remember "the word" as part of a catchy rhyme played on radio stations advertising Thunderbird, a sweet, peppermint-flavored wine:

"What's the word?"
"Thunderbird!"
"What's the price?"
"Thirty twice."
"Another nickel'll get you ice."

When y'ats enter Incarnate Word Church, they may be thinking Word-Made-Flesh; on the other hand, they may be thinking about their computers or a swig of T-Bird wine.

Readers of John Kennedy Toole's *A Confederacy of Dunces* should not go looking around New Orleans for the church of St. Odo of Cluny, the parish church of the novel's antihero, Ignatius Reilly. Unfortunately, the church of St. Odo of Cluny is just as fictional as the buffoonish Ignatius. However, there really is a St. Odo of Cluny. He was a tenth-century Benedictine monk, abbot, and leader of a reform movement.

Some church parishes in the archdiocese define their neighborhoods. St. Dominic's Church on Harrison Avenue, for example, *is* Lakeview. Corpus Christi Parish *is* the Seventh Ward. St. Agnes Parish *is* Old Jefferson. A y'at's answer to the question, "Where do you live?" could be interchangeably, "Lakeview," or, "St. Dominic's Parish."

To be a Complete Y'at Catholic, you must occasionally attend a Mass, baptism, wedding, or special ceremony at the spiritual and physical heart of New Orleans Catholicism, St. Louis Cathedral, better known simply as "The Cathedral." Before entering The Cathedral, it is best to walk through the earthy, exotic, entertaining world of the Vieux Carré. Across Jackson Square from The Cathedral, the beignets are frying, the café au lait is steaming, and the tourists are getting powdered sugar on their clothes. As the aroma from Café du Monde rolls across the square, it mixes with the smells of the mules lined up to pull carriages of visitors along the streets of the French Quarter. The way to the door of The Cathedral is lined with mimes, portrait artists, tarot-card readers, jugglers and musicians as well as people taking pictures of them. As the bell tolls in the tower of The Cathedral, ships on the Mississippi River sound reverberating blasts on their horns. With the senses thoroughly stimulated, the faithful are ready for Mass.

Inside The Cathedral, the flags and murals stand out. Above the altar is St. Louis, leading the knights into the

Seventh Crusade, as the mural explains in French (*St. Louis, Roi de France, Annonce La 7eme Croisade*). This is a curious scene to honor the patron saint of New Orleans, the state of Louisiana, and indeed the entire Mississippi valley. Louis IX's sanctity comes from his almsgiving, care of the sick, founding of hospitals, and building of cathedrals. His military expedition in the Seventh Crusade was a disaster. Even before he reached the Holy Land, Louis and his army, which had degenerated into an ugly bunch of looters, were defeated at a battle in Egypt. The Arabs took Louis prisoner and extracted a large ransom for his release. He managed to get to Palestine and visited the holy shrines that were available to Christians, but his military campaign was a failure. He tried a crusade again several years later, only to die of disease in Tunis in North Africa before ever reaching the Holy Land. Some of the stained-glass windows in The Cathedral do, however, show Louis building the famous church of St. Chapelle and helping out a leper, in addition to his crusading.

The Cathedral dates from 1795, during the Spanish colonial period. Before that date only a parish church stood on the site facing Bienville's Place d'Armes, now Jackson Square. The first bishop of The Cathedral was Luis Ignacio Maria de Peñalver y Cardenas. Names got easier by the twentieth century, when Archbishops James Blenk and John Shaw succeeded to the chair first held by the worthy Luis Ignacio Maria de Peñalver y Cardenas.

Once a year Mass is celebrated in The Cathedral in the language of St. Louis's native land. The French Mass is held on the Sunday nearest Bastille Day, July 14, the French national holiday. This is a curious if not ironic day to be worshiping God in a church dedicated to a saintly king. Bastille Day was the beginning of the French Revolution, a

violent and aggressive attack on the existing order in
France, especially against the royalty and church. The
leaders of the French Revolution were militant atheists.
They destroyed churches, killed clergy and aristocrats,
and declared atheism the state religion. The French who
settled Louisiana before the 1760s were prerevolutionary
and monarchial. In 1763, Louisiana was transferred to
Spain, also Catholic and monarchial, long before the
French Revolution of 1789. The tricolor flag of revolutionary France flew over New Orleans for just a few days in
1803 until Napoleon Bonaparte, one of those atheistic
Frenchmen, sold Louisiana to the United States.
Nevertheless, New Orleans celebrates its French Catholic
heritage with a Mass in a cathedral dedicated to a saintly
king on the day the revolutionaries began their efforts to
destroy the French church and the monarchy. Some
Frenchmen believe that God, if he exists, is French. New
Orleanians humor these French people and treat them
with kindness, but New Orleanians know that God is a y'at.

CHAPTER 5

Theology

With churches, saints' names, and other reminders of Catholicism everywhere in New Orleans, it is no wonder that y'ats are very expressive of their religion and not embarrassed to use theological terms freely. These manifestations of faith are usually verbal, although expressions of faith are sometimes posted in the classified section of the daily newspaper, in and on automobiles, or even in barrooms.

God aka The Supreme Being

The Supreme Being, the creator of the universe, identified as God the Father, is called by y'ats simply "God" (pronounced *GAWD*). The Deity's presence is acknowledged in daily conversations in such expressions as, "Oh, Gawd!" or the reminder that the Creator is a judge of moral behavior with, "Gawd sees you doin' that." The veracity of a statement one y'at makes to another is often authenticated with the emphatic oath, "I swear t' Gawd!" Sometimes when misfortune falls upon someone doing something bad, a y'at will declare solemnly, "Gawd don't like ugly." Y'ats know that the Supreme Being is judgmental but just. The omnipotence of the Supreme Being is also frequently witnessed to by y'ats with such pious exclamations as, "Gawd Almighty! The traffic on the I-10 is terrible!"

Y'ats also frequently are heard to express their profound belief in the divinity of Jesus. No y'at would ever be confused with a Unitarian. The doctrine that Jesus is the Son of God who is also God, the second person of the Trinity, breaks no theological sweat on the y'at brow. The exclamation "Jesus God!" (pronounced *JEE-zuz GAWD*) used freely by y'ats even when they are not in an ecclesiastical or spiritual setting, is vigorous testimony to the faith professed for more than eighteen hundred years in the Nicene Creed. Y'ats can be heard making such professions of faith as, "Jesus Gawd! Li'l Eddie spent all Mama's bingo money at the casino." Or, "Jesus Gawd! It's rainin' so hard I need to move the car to the neutral ground so it won't get flooded." Y'at piety is also shown by the use of the Lord's name with his New Testament title, as in "Jesus Christ! The hurricane's comin' right for us!" Occasionally a y'at will invoke his full name, including middle initial, by exclaiming "Jesus H. Christ!" but no one knows for sure what the *H* stands for or when, where, why, or how it got stuck into the Lord's name. Perhaps it is another of those unfathomable theological mysteries that y'ats do not question.

God the Father and Jesus, God the Son, are the first and second persons, respectively, of the Blessed Trinity. The Holy Spirit, identified as the third person, gets less attention from y'at Catholics. The Spirit, in the words of the Nicene Creed, proceeds from the Father and the Son. The term "Holy Spirit" is a recent theological name change. With Vatican II, Church officials decided that the English translation of *Spiritus Sanctus,* the Holy Ghost, was both archaic and tended to make the third person of the Trinity into some sort of Halloween character. Emulating the Anglicans, who were already using English in their liturgies, the post-Vatican II bishops changed the Holy Ghost's name to Holy Spirit. Could the bishops also have been aware of 1950s "jive" talk on the streets of New Orleans that expressed the mystical union of the Trinity as "Big Daddy, J.C., and the Spook"? The name change went only so far because Holy Ghost Church in New Orleans is still Holy Ghost Church. Y'ats prefer stability in their theology. However, in making the sign of the cross, y'ats do invoke the Father, Son, and Holy Spirit; the Holy Ghost rarely gets mention there anymore. In a manifestation of the name change, there is a post-Vatican II church in New Orleans on the lower coast of Algiers that is dedicated to the Holy Spirit.

A discussion of New Orleans and the Trinity is not complete without a word about food. In fact, it is nearly impossible to discuss anything about New Orleans without mentioning food. If the term "Holy Trinity" is spoken outside of a church, chances are that the y'at using it and the y'ats hearing it are thinking food. To be specific, in cooking, the Holy Trinity is the combination of three vegetables that are essential ingredients in Creole cooking—onion, celery, and bell pepper. Recipes and directions in Creole cooking usually start with the familiar mantra, "First you make a roux." A roux is made by heating cooking oil or butter in a heavy black pot or skillet, adding white flour, and browning it to the desired degree of darkness. At the moment the color is right, you add the Holy Trinity and stir mightily to cool the roux and prevent the flour from darkening more or burning. The direction, "First you make a roux," is thus inaccurate. Recipes should recognize the theological primacy of the Trinity by stating, "First you chop up the Holy Trinity." If the Holy Trinity is not chopped first, when the roux reaches the right shade of brown, it is too late to start chopping. The roux will burn even if the pot is removed from the fire. There may be some theological symbolism here: The punishing fires of hell are cooled and quenched by the presence of the Holy Trinity.

If the roux is to be used with stewed vegetables, snap beans or cabbage for example, the roux should be browned lightly, to about the color of the uniform worn by a school boy at a New Orleans Catholic school, sort of a khaki. As a base for gumbo made from poultry and sausage, the roux should be browned until it reaches the color of dark-roast New Orleans coffee grounds. Then the Holy Trinity is added.

Belief in the Trinity is also demonstrated in the traditional method of flavoring a New Orleans snowball. Another of the many skewed realities in the culture of the Crescent City is the fact that a snowball has no snow in it and is not a ball. This hot-weather concoction is made from shaved, not crushed, ice covered with sweet, flavored syrup and is usually served in a cup or in a take-out container like those used in Chinese restaurants. The original New Orleans snowball was served on a paper plate, but the practice gave way to the cone cups. Elsewhere in America this summer cooler is called a snow cone, but in New Orleans, devoid as it is of snow, the original term "snowball" has continued. One of the oldest and most popular snowball stands is Hansen's. The matriarch of the family explained that each snowball gets three shakes of syrup from the dispenser, one for the Father, one for the Son, and one for the Holy Ghost. Waiting to eat a snowball on a sweltering August afternoon, you can readily believe in the existence of hell, and a few spoonfuls of a snowball should return your thoughts to Trinitarian theology.

Mary aka the B.V.M.

Mary, the mother of Jesus, gets a lot of attention in y'at Catholicism. Many, many churches are dedicated to her. From Our Lady of Perpetual Help in the suburb of Kenner to Holy Name of Mary in Algiers Point to Mater Dolorosa (pronounced *MAH-duh DULL-a-rosa*) in Carrollton, devotion to Mother Mary is widespread. When the city of New Orleans was expanding in the late eighteenth century, a section upriver from the Vieux Carré was developed as the Faubourg Ste. Marie, now called the Faubourg St. Mary. Of course there is no church honoring Mary in the Faubourg St. Mary, and St. Mary Street is much farther uptown. There are churches honoring virtually every aspect of what theologians call Marian theology. There is also coverage of the ethnic and national devotions to her in the churches of Our Lady of Guadalupe, Our Lady Queen of Vietnam, and Our Lady of Lourdes. Our Lady of the Lake faces Lake Pontchartrain on the north shore in Mandeville. The church of The Visitation of Our Lady commemorates Mary's arrival at the home of her cousin, Elizabeth, and each telling the other that she is pregnant. Our Lady Star of the Sea church originally ministered to fishermen's families. Mary's parents are honored with St. Ann's in the suburb of Metairie and St. Joachim's in the swamps of Barataria.

The church namers must have liked superlative adjectives. Although the beautiful church on Esplanade Avenue is Our Lady of the Rosary, better known as Holy Rosary,

when the archdiocese built a new church upriver from
New Orleans in Hahnville, it was dedicated to Our Lady of
the Most Holy Rosary. Why was it necessary to add those
adjectives? There is a legend that Our Lady gave the
rosary to St. Dominic; wouldn't the origin of the gift make
the rosary holy? Is there a difference between a rosary, a
holy rosary, and a most holy rosary? Is there a non-holy
rosary around? Answers to these difficult theological
inquiries will have to be found elsewhere.

On Louisiana Avenue is a church dedicated to Our Lady
of Good Counsel, but there is no explanation why, when,
where, or how Mary became a lawyer. Her son did not
mince words in his criticisms of members of the legal pro-
fession, which adds to the mystery. Perhaps Mary's title as
"Good Counsel" is a sign of hope for lawyers that they, too,
can be saved.

The most important title given to Mary in New Orleans is
Our Lady of Prompt Succor (pronounced *PROM SUCK-ah*).
In this title, Our Lady is the protectress of all that is good
and holy and not so good or not so holy in the city of y'ats.
Our Lady's protection was sought in an all-night prayer vigil
before the Battle of New Orleans, fought on January 8,
1815, in the sugar-cane fields in Chalmette, six miles downriver from the French Quarter. In late 1814, as the War of
1812 was winding down and diplomats were gathered in
Paris to end the conflict, the British tried to seize New
Orleans and the Mississippi River to solidify their hold on
North America. They probed the marshes east of the city
and tried coming up the river, but they were not successful.
General Andrew Jackson frantically assembled a rag-tag
army to repel the invasion. Anticipating multiculturalism
by almost two hundred years, he formed a force of regular
American troops; backwoodsmen from Tennessee and

Kentucky; local, French-speaking militia, including Creoles of color; and smugglers and privateers operating under the direction Jean and Pierre Lafitte. The British, having been unsuccessful in their attempts to reach the city, drew up a battle plan to advance in European field formation and to march on the city with their overwhelming numbers of well-trained troops. As the redcoats approached and General Jackson set up a defensive line at Chalmette, the women of the city gathered with the Ursuline nuns to pray to Our Lady of Prompt Succor to spare their city. All night January 7-8, 1815, the fearful women prayed, begging Notre Dame de Prompt Secours for victory over the invaders.

Holy Mother Mary, not usually known for her military prowess or bloodthirsty tactics, came through the next morning. General Jackson and his polyglot soldiers destroyed the British army, killing thousands of them, including their commanding general. The survivors retreated back to their waiting ships, set sail, and left North America forever. The Americans had very few casualties, and the victory made General Jackson a national hero.

Jackson did not entirely trust the local militia who helped achieve victory. He thought the French-speaking Catholics might break and run as the redcoats advanced. He did not place the New Orleans militia in the line of battle, setting them on the flank instead. Despite his snub to the bravery of the local Catholic soldiers, Our Lady of Prompt Succor's protection benefited General Jackson's political career. Without his victory on January 8, 1815, he would never have become president—and he was a Protestant!

The deliverance of the city of New Orleans by Our Lady of Prompt Succor is an event commemorated every year

Devotion to Our Lady is enhanced by plastic flowers and Carnival beads.

since 1815. The archbishop celebrates Mass in the National Shrine of Our Lady of Prompt Succor on the campus of Ursuline Academy, thanking the Holy Mother for protection from destruction. The effectiveness of the devotion for the past almost two hundred years is readily apparent in the fact that no British army has ever come close to New Orleans since. Because of the effectiveness of Our Lady's protection, y'ats also seek her help when hurricanes threaten. Well-organized y'ats have hurricane-preparedness check lists that include such items as batteries, candles, canned food, a portable radio, and prayers to Our Lady of Prompt Succor. Although there were thousands of prayers to Our Lady of Prompt Succor before Hurricane Katrina, they were not enough. Perhaps y'ats have asked too much from their patroness for too long.

A grateful city remembered the effectiveness of the prayers of the Ursuline nuns that saved the city. They were forever granted free rides on the public transportation system. This free-ride largess was later extended to all nuns in habits, probably because bus drivers and streetcar operators could not tell the difference between the various orders of nuns, even though they wore different habits. No one ever raised the issue of separation of church and state, even though the sisters rode free on streetcars and buses subsidized with taxpayers' money. However, as the nuns shifted from traditional habits to civilian dress and as the public transportation system became a true public agency, the free-ride for Our Lady of Prompt Succor's supporters was no more.

Although Our Lady of Prompt Succor has protected the city well from invading redcoats and, for the most part, hurricanes, she was not paying close attention to her own shrine. A few years ago, the annual January 8 Mass of thanksgiving to her at the shrine at Ursuline Academy was threatened by an invasion of termites, which closed down the chapel. The archdiocese shifted the Mass to the church of Our Lady of Prompt Succor in Chalmette, much closer to the site of the 1815 battle. The battle against the termites was apparently successful because the annual Mass returned to the shrine at Ursuline Academy the next year.

In the 1950s and early 1960s, New Orleans musicians were nationally popular. Led by Fats Domino with his bandleader, Dave Bartholomew, and influenced by rhythm-and-blues progenitor Professor Longhair, New Orleans music was becoming nationally recognized at the beginning of the rock-and-roll era. But New Orleans musicians were not as alert as Andy Jackson and the New Orleanians of 1814, because a British invasion began in 1964 that overwhelmed them. This was the "British Invasion" of popular music led by The Beatles. There was no public prayer to Our Lady of Prompt Succor in 1964 as there was in 1815; the British invaded and conquered. The Beatles even played a concert in New Orleans.

The American public's taste in popular music is, to say the least, fickle, and New Orleans rhythm and blues, after languishing in obscurity, returned to popularity many years after the British Invasion. Who knows—maybe Our Lady of Prompt Succor could hear, from her shrine on State Street, Professor Longhair's long fingers ripping out "Tipitina" on his piano, or Fats Domino's "Ain't That a Shame."

In 1981, an event occurred in a place so far away and so small that no y'at had ever heard of it. Mary appeared for the first time that year to some children in the town of Medjugorje, in Bosnia-Herzegovina, then part of Yugoslavia. Medjugorje was a Catholic enclave in a Muslim-majority province. There were further apparitions, and news of the apparitions reached New Orleans. At first, just a few of the Marian faithful went to Medjugorje, partly out of curiosity, party out of desperation for some personal crisis, partly out of pure devotion to Our Lady. They returned with news that, although they had not actually seen an apparition of Mary, they had seen strange and wonderful signs in the sky. There were reports of seeing the sun "dance." The principal emotion that visitors to Medjugorje experienced was a sense of peace and calm, and they believed that Mother Mary had appeared to them in that fashion.

The stories of Medjugorje and the apparitions became the religious topic among y'at Catholics. Travel agencies began booking whole tours to Medjugorje. Y'ats who had never heard of Yugoslavia, let alone Bosnia-Herzegovina, were getting onto airplanes, some for the first time, to travel a third of the way around the world. The travel industry was delighted; New Orleanians who had never been any farther from home than Biloxi or Baton Rouge became world travelers in groups. Our Lady was certainly smiling on those who were making a living selling airplane tickets and booking hotel rooms.

But there were problems in Medjugorje. The local Catholic bishop there did not accept the children's reports of visions of Mary as authentic. He apparently did not see the sun dance, as others had done. The Vatican deferred to the local bishop and did not endorse the apparitions as true. None of these actions and inactions had any effect on the y'at believers. They continued to visit Medjugorje, some returning for several pilgrimages. Most were very satisfied, thankful for having made the journey and experiencing the sense of peace and harmony for which they credited Mary. The lack of a stamp of approval by the institutional church was not a problem for them. They felt the presence of the

Holy Mother even if the local bishop and priests did not. The pilgrimages ended when Bosnia descended into a horrible ethnic war between the Serbs of Bosnia, whose religious identity is rooted in the Serbian Orthodox Church, and the Muslim Bosnians.

Holy Mother Mary has a shrine in Mid-City unlike any other. In a combination bowling alley and live-music night spot, a picture of Mary greets bowlers and bar patrons as they ascend a steep flight of stairs. The stair climb to Mid-City Rock 'n' Bowl reminds you of the many European shrines that require a good bit of stair-climbing effort to see a statue of the Virgin. Montserrat in northeastern Spain, near Barcelona, is a good example. Pilgrims must ascend many steps to view a smoky, black effigy of the Holy Mother. The picture of Mary in such a noisy, happy atmosphere as Rock 'n' Bowl makes the first-time visitor wonder whether Mary has been named patroness of bowling. The smiling proprietor, John Blancher, says that the highly popular business was an answer to prayers he and his wife made to Mary many years earlier. In the fall of 1988, Blancher and his wife made a pilgrimage to Medjugorje along with many other y'ats, both the devout and the curious. Blancher did not have any particular unusual experience there, but he left a written petition to Mary on an altar where he prayed to acquire a business that would involve his whole family. This petition was based on a dream that he had had for a long time. A few weeks after returning from Medjugorje, someone asked him if he wanted to buy a shabby, old bowling alley that was owned by the Knights of Columbus. On All Saints Day, November 1, 1988, a very appropriate day for a y'at Catholic, he opened for business. Things did not go well at first, but when he got the idea of live music inside the bowling alley, he came upon a combination that has made Rock 'n' Bowl one of the most popular, friendliest night spots in the city of New Orleans. In thanksgiving for an answer to his prayer at Medjugorje, Blancher posted a picture of Our Lady at the top of the stairs so that every visitor, customer, musician, and delivery person sees the image of Mary upon arrival. Is that devotion or what?

Rock 'n' Bowl also observes January 8 as a feast day. Although January 8, the date of the Battle of New Orleans, is the Feast of Our Lady of Prompt Succor, it is also the birthday of America's most popular secular saint, Elvis Presley. Every year on the Feast of Our Lady of Prompt Succor, St. Elvis of Graceland makes an appearance at Rock 'n' Bowl. A y'at can make Mass at the Shrine of Our Lady of Prompt Succor in the morning and see an apparition of Elvis in the evening.

Sin

In the realm of moral theology, y'at Catholics have what can generously be described as a laissez-faire attitude toward the Seven Deadly Sins. The Seven Deadly Sins are Pride, Covetousness, Lust, Envy, Gluttony, Anger, and Sloth. The best guess is that they originated in the medieval morality plays that were designed to scare the superstitious faithful into walking the straight and narrow path. These sins, it should be observed, are not indigenous to New Orleans and often seem to be at odds with what y'ats see as positive spiritual experiences.

To begin with Pride, for many years y'ats drove around with bumper stickers on their cars that proclaimed "Pride Builds New Orleans." Later, an anti-litter campaign to prevent the dumping of trash into coastal waterways created bumper stickers reading "Take Pride Gulf-wide." More recently, bumper stickers that state "New Orleans: Proud to Call It Home" have been attached to vehicles. How can a y'at sin by making the city a better place to live? Covetousness is inherent to y'ats. It is not a sin, it is a characteristic of birth. No Carnival parade could function without covetousness. There is no rational reason that anyone, y'at or not, would want all those beads, doubloons, plastic toys, and other stuff tossed by the thousands of masked riders aboard parade floats. Y'ats and their imitators scream and yell and roll in the dirt to satisfy some strong compulsion to possess things that have no use or purpose whatsoever other than the act of acquisition itself. Covetousness is a necessary attribute of the y'at. That is to say, if you aren't trying to get your hands on some Mardi Gras beads, you're not a y'at.

Lust. Bourbon Street. Need I say more? Although most y'ats do not regularly frequent the fleshpots of Bourbon Street, they readily acknowledge that, in a city whose livelihood is dependent on tourists spending money, Bourbon Street, however tawdry and tacky, draws in many, many outsiders with money to spend. Lust is thus a major industry whether the locals visit the sleazy joints or not. Furthermore, commercial lust in New Orleans has been a major industry for a very long time. In 1897, in order to control the widespread prostitution throughout the city, the New Orleans City Council created America's first legalized red-light district. It was called Storyville, a dubious honor for City Councilman Sidney Story, who had proposed the legislation. For twenty years, thousands of pimps and whores, sailors and "johns" made lust big, legitimate business. That it is also sinful seems to have been unimportant. Lust is part of the history of the Crescent City.

Envy also has an ambiguous place in the spiritual life of New Orleans. The citizens of the city take pride in the fact that their police department is the envy of the world in the difficult task of controlling crowds. Other cities look with awe and envy as the New Orleans Police Department, with apparent ease and good cheer, keeps the raucous, heavy-drinking crowds of Carnival season under control without becoming heavy-handed. On the other hand, New Orleans business people look wistfully and with envy to other cities like Atlanta and Memphis that seem to attract better industries and higher-paying jobs. Envy is perhaps more a part of the cultural landscape than a deadly sin.

Gluttony? In New Orleans? Who's kidding whom? Even more than Lust, Gluttony is a major industry. It is also a revered characteristic of y'ats. No y'at was the least bit surprised and perhaps was even proud when a national study, obviously conducted by some prissy nutrition Nazis, declared that New Orleans was America's fattest city. The announcement was toasted in many bars and eateries throughout the city. When the Crescent City fell from first place the following year, some y'ats were in disbelief and figured the judges were bribed.

The sin of Anger is when it is inappropriate and directed at someone who has done no wrong. Bad anger occurs when someone at a St. Patrick's Day parade becomes angry because the float riders, holding cabbages in both hands, refuse the suppliant's plea for free vegetables. Despite a common misconception among some y'ats, there is no God-given right to catch free stuff, including cabbages, from parade floats. The rejection of the cabbage-plea should be an occasion to exhort the riders on the next float even more loudly, possibly even plying them with a can of cold beer held aloft. A parade is definitely not a time for anger, even if the person standing next to you manages to snare those good long beads that a float rider was aiming directly to you. A pious y'at knows that real anger at a parade is always sinful because it violates the holy principle of everybody having a good time. Righteous anger is appropriate and is not sinful, especially in such solemn occasions as when a person eating a piece of king cake bites into the plastic baby in the cake and tries to hide the fact from the rest of the people in the office.

Y'ats are often accused by outsiders of being lazy. These snobbish prigs like to point out that the economic condition of New Orleans is chronically bad and that locals are not interested in working hard to make the good middle-class wages that would bring the city away from the edge of poverty and into the economic mainstream of America. There is much evidence to support these observations, and y'ats can become defensive about the low economic status of the metropolitan area, depending as it does primarily on tourists' dollars. Sloth and laziness are, however, often in the eye of the beholder. The popular culture of New Orleans has always had disdain for or cheerful rejection of what the rest of the country knows as the Protestant work ethic.

Many of the movers and shakers of the city, the bankers and lawyers and other business executives, observed a practice as civilized as Frenchmen sipping Pernod in cafés along the Champs-Élysées—the tradition of The Friday Lunch. Leaving their offices about noon on Friday, these fat cats gather at Galatoire's, Arnaud's, Antoine's, and other such restaurants. These gatherings are not the equivalent of the "power lunch" popular in other big cities at which the professional class discusses business, sizes each other up, and exchanges industry gossip. Rather, New

Orleans Friday Lunch topics include more important matters such as food, renovations at the yacht club, wine,
developments happening on the Mississippi Gulf Coast,
and fishing. With the nationalization and globalization of
business requiring professional y'ats to spend more time
on their phones and at their computers, the Friday lunch
tradition is somewhat in decline, a turn of events lamented
by many true New Orleanians. Therein lies the perception
of sloth. New Orleanians are anything but slothful when
truly important issues are involved. Carnival and food are
at the top of the list. Business and work are the means of
providing the wherewithal so that y'ats can spend freely on
their most revered institutions. The following true story is
illustrative.

In February 1984, construction on the World's Fair was
not only in full swing, it was a little behind schedule. On
the Friday before Mardi Gras a foreman assembled his
crew in the afternoon to inform them that it would be necessary to work on Saturday and Sunday, ten hours each
day. The workers' union contract provided that they would
receive double hourly wages for work done on weekends.
That meant that the twenty hours worked that weekend
would be the equivalent of another week's work. This
should have been a very attractive proposition to men who
knew that they would be out of work when the World's Fair
opened in May. But there are priorities that go beyond
work, and celebrating Mardi Gras is one of them. One of
the construction crew members declined the weekend
work without hesitation explaining, "I'm marching on
Mardi Gras with the Wild Tchoupitoulas. I gotta work on
my suit!" The Wild Tchoupitoulas is a tribe of Mardi Gras
Indians, and preparing the suit, the elaborate costume
worn on the march through the streets of the city, is the

most important activity a tribe member can perform. The rejection of additional employment in such circumstance cannot be considered sloth. First things come first.

The y'at attitude toward the moral questions presented by the Seven Deadly Sins is a sort-of indirect, unintentional, passive manifestation of Pelagianism, an attractive old heresy. Pelagius was an Anglo-Saxon monk who lived at the end of the fourth century and the beginning of the fifth century. He created a stir when he went to Italy and North Africa and preached that human beings were basically good, the commission of sin was a personal choice, and God's grace was unnecessary for salvation. There is no Original Sin that inclines people to evil, he taught. He found himself in conflict with the great St. Augustine, whose theology vigorously accepted Original Sin and the tendency of people toward evil. Augustine's doctrine prevailed. Pelagianism was condemned by the Council of Carthage in 418 and Council of Ephesus in 431. Yet vestiges of Pelagius's doctrine may be apparent in the laissez-faire attitude of y'ats toward personal moral transgressions. The Seven Deadly Sins are personal decisions, not inherent inclinations in the practice of y'at Catholicism. Like Pelagius, y'ats believe that people are inherently good and want to express that goodness in celebration.

CHAPTER 6

Sacraments, Devotions, Holidays, Feast Days, and Other Events

Baptism aka Christening

The beginning of Christian life is the sacrament of Baptism. Baptism is an important event for y'ats, even those who are not regular churchgoers. Baptizing an infant involves many rituals beyond taking the baby to church and having the priest pour water over the child's head while the kid makes a lot of noise and the adults laugh. The first thing to do in planning a y'at baptism, even before checking with the priest, is to line up some godparents. In y'at Catholicism, the godparents are traditionally identified by French terms. The godfather is *parrain,* and that honor may become his title or name for all the children in the family, even those for who are not his godchildren. Indeed, there are many men in New Orleans for whom Parrain is the name by which they are known in their neighborhoods and businesses. The French word for godmother is *marraine,* but that term is rarely used anymore. Instead, the diminutive form from Creole French, *nanan,* is given to the godmother, and the term is shortened even more to nan, nanny, or nonny.

Finding appropriate godparents can sometimes be difficult. They are, by Church rule, supposed to be active

Catholics in good standing, and finding people who meet the letter of canon law may be a challenge. When choosing a *parrain,* the parents of the infant should be careful to pick someone who will not show up at church with a weaving walk and fumes wafting through his slurred speech. Likewise, a *nanan* with too much cleavage revealing the tattoos on her bosom does not display the proper spirit of the sacrament of reception into Christian life. Y'at parents are wise to bring to the church, along with the diaper bag and a bottle, breath mints for *parrain* and a shawl for *nanan.*

Choosing a church for the baptism can be a source of conflict and stress for y'ats. The archdiocese allows Catholics to be baptized in any church, as long as the arrangements are made with the pastor. The infant's mother may feel compelled to have her child christened in the church where she and her mother were baptized. The father may also feel the need to continue a family tradition in another church. Grandmothers have to be soothed and feelings have to be taken into consideration. Sometimes the christening is delayed until the ruffled feathers smooth out and family members are at least smiling at each other.

Many y'at families have a traditional baptismal garment that has been used for generations. It is usually a long white embroidered gown with a matching cap. It is used by both boys and girls, whose gender is shown by pink or blue ribbons. After the actual baptism ceremony, guests and family members gather around to admire the child and the gown with such comments as, "Gawd, ain't she precious?" and "Look at that gown. I remember when your mama wore it when she was christened." It is inevitable that a deceased relative will be mentioned. "It's too bad Ma-maw's gone and can't see the baby. He would have been her fo'teenth great-grandchild." Right there in that statement is the essence of the Christian doctrine of baptism—death and new life in Jesus. Y'ats inherently understand the mystical continuity.

Matrimony

The sacrament of Matrimony is also a time of great celebration. There is an old belief in New Orleans that a woman planning to get married should book a reception hall even before she has a prospective groom because the most popular reception halls are booked sometimes years in advance, especially on Saturdays in the spring. The archdiocese is also agreeable to the desires of couples to be married in any church. Once the rule was that the wedding should take place in the bride's parish church, but the archdiocese allows the sacrament of Matrimony to be administered in any parish church that will permit it. Some of the more popular churches are as busy as the reception halls and have lots of restrictions. The church must be booked early, too, again maybe even before the groom is selected. Certain priests get reputations for performing very joyous and spiritually uplifting wedding ceremonies. They, too, are in demand and need to be scheduled well in advance.

The archdiocese is *not* permissive about wedding masses outside a church building. Couples who dream about a ceremony under the oaks in Audubon Park or at the New Orleans Museum of Art cannot have it done by the church. This restriction causes much grief, and those Catholics who are less committed to the institutional church sometimes seek other options. One of these is the availability of former priests who have gone into the wedding business.

In Catholic theology a priest's ordination cannot be rescinded. At ordination he is solemnly reminded that *tu es sacerdos semper,* you are a priest forever. Even after the priest is officially "laicized," that is, relieved of his priestly duties when he departs the official priesthood, he still retains the power to administer the sacraments. Further, the theology of matrimony is that the sacrament is not something that the priest performs on the couple, but it is a spiritual bond that the couple convey to each other. The priest is the one who performs the ceremony to give the sacrament validity under canon law. Therefore, the former priest can perform a theologically valid marriage even if the wedding is illicit under church law. This ecclesiastical loophole provides an opportunity for enterprising former priests to have a second job on Saturdays and other times away from their day jobs. Whether the couple considers themselves validly married within the church is a personal matter, but y'ats who really, really want to be married at some place that is very special in their relationship—the Flying Horses at City Park, for example—cannot have an active priest perform the wedding.

After the motorcycle police have escorted the wedding party from the church to the reception hall and the party begins, there are some essential points of a y'at wedding that come forth. The first is oyster patties. It seems that no y'at wedding reception is complete without a server with a tray full of tiny pastry shells filled with oysters chopped and cooked with herbs and butter. Most reception halls do a pretty good job preparing this vital part of the wedding. Some do it extremely well, and there are some places whose oyster patties are so ghastly that a guest at the reception may pause and wonder whether the marriage is actually valid. It is almost as embarrassing as the story in the Bible about the wedding in Cana where they ran out of wine and Mary had to ask Jesus to create some more. When choosing a reception hall, a prospective bride should always check around for the establishment's reputation for oyster patties.

Novenas and Other Special Devotions

The novena is alive and well in y'at Catholicism. Although this devotional practice has slipped into decline in many places following the changes of Vatican II, y'ats, who are nothing if not traditional, continue to perform novenas. The word "novena" is Latin, meaning nine each. A novena consists of a set of prayers, sometimes said in conjunction with Mass, for nine days. The significance of the number nine in Catholic theology is unclear. The devotion of nine days of prayer is a very ancient practice originating with the pagan Greeks and Romans. They observed nine days of mourning following a death or burial. Nine is also associated with the devotion to the Sacred Heart of Jesus, observed by Mass and prayers on the first Friday of nine consecutive months.

This is as good a place as any to outline the numerology of Catholic theology. Perhaps the numbers are no more than identifying marks. Some, like the novena, may have historical or mystical significance. Beginning with one, the concept of One God is expressed in the Nicene Creed. Jesus has two distinct natures, being true God and true man, also explicitly stated in the Nicene Creed. The number three is expressed by the Holy Trinity, and the four Gospels of Matthew, Mark, Luke, and John come next. Some Catholics still have a devotion to the Five Most Precious Wounds suffered by Jesus at his crucifixion: nail holes in his hands and feet and a wound in his side where he was pierced after death. There are six principal rules of church law, called the precepts or commandments of the church. They are attendance at Mass on Sundays and Holy Days of Obligation and to refrain from servile work on those days; fasting and abstinence on the days assigned; recieving the sacrament of reconciliation at least once a year; receiving the sacrament of the Eucharist at least once a year during the Easter season; contributing to the support of the church; and not marrying a relative within a forbidden degree of consanguinity or having a solemn marriage at times forbidden by the church.

Number seven is the sacraments, officially designated by the Council of Trent in response to the Reformation and Martin Luther, who said there were only two sacraments. The Catholic sacraments are Baptism, Confirmation, Reconciliation or Penance, Holy Eucharist, Matrimony, Holy Orders, and Anointing of the Sick (formerly called Extreme Unction and pronounced *EX-tree MUNK-shun* by y'ats).

The eight Beatitudes spoken by Jesus in his Sermon on the Mount ("Blessed are ...) are some of the best-known passages in the New Testament. Number Nine has many mystical and numerological significances. In addition to the novena and the nine first Fridays, there are the nine choirs of angels: angels, archangels, cherubim, seraphim, powers, thrones, dominations, virtues, and principalities. Everyone is familiar with the Ten Commandments, even if they haven't seen the movie. There were eleven faithful apostles left after Judas betrayed Jesus and then committed suicide. Just as there were twelve tribes of Israel, there were originally twelve apostles as well as twelve baskets of leftovers after Jesus had fed the hungry with bread and fish by the Sea of Galilee. After Judas was gone, a thirteenth apostle was added to Jesus' inner circle, a man named Mathias. The devotion of the way of the cross consists of fourteen stations commemorating the journey of Jesus from receiving his death sentence to his crucifixion, death, and burial. Number fifteen counts the mysteries of the rosary, five each of the Joyful Mysteries, Sorrowful Mysteries, and Glorious Mysteries.

Enough of Catholic numerology and back to novenas. Devotion to the Sacred Heart of Jesus (pronounced *SAY-Crid HAWT*) is still popular in y'at Catholicism. In addition to a Canal Street church dedicated to the Sacred Heart, there is a fashionable and excellent high school for girls by that name. The novena to the Sacred Heart is a continuation of an ancient and mystical cult that makes the object of devotion the physical heart of Jesus the God-man. The belief is that Jesus' physical heart manifests God's great love in becoming a human being and sacrificing himself for the sins of all. Jesus' Sacred Heart is depicted in art in the familiar painting showing Christ with an open, flaming chest in the center of which burns an anatomically correct heart, ringed by a circle of thorns, with flame at the top, a powerful image of the Lord's burning love for humankind. The Feast of the Sacred Heart is the Friday following the Feast of Corpus Christi, now given an English name, the Feast of the Body and Blood of Christ. Corpus Christi is the second Sunday after Pentecost, and therefore usually in June. The nine days of prayer begin on the following Friday, and the nine first Fridays usually start then, too.

When the House of Blues, a nightclub on Decatur Street, first opened in New Orleans, there were accusations that the logo of the establishment was a sacrilegious parody of the image of the Sacred Heart of Jesus. The House of Blues'

Y'ats offer prayers and novenas to the Sacred Heart of Jesus, which should not be confused with the logo of the House of Blues.

symbol is at first glance very similar to the burning heart in the pictures of the Sacred Heart. The owners of the club made some changes so that its symbol does not look exactly like the Sacred Heart of Jesus, but the club's Web site refers to the symbol as "The Sacred Heart." So what's the matter with somebody saying a novena to the Sacred Heart in a nightclub?

Another novena popular with y'ats, especially women, is the novena to St. Ann. Ann was Mary's mother and thus the grandmother of Jesus or, as a y'at might say, Jesus' maw-maw. St. Ann does not appear in any of the four gospels considered authentic by the Catholic Church, that is, that they were undoubtedly inspired by God. Ann shows up in the apocryphal Gospel of James. Although the document is not considered divinely inspired, the Gospel of James is not considered to be fictitious. Ann is one of the few female saints on the liturgical calendar who is not a martyr, virgin, nun, or queen. She is a wife, mother, and grandmother, and some y'ats think that such status is in itself good enough for sainthood. Matriarchal devotion is a hallmark of y'at society. Novenas to St. Ann are held at the National Shrine of St. Ann in Metairie. St. Ann, whose husband was St. Joachim, is the saint single women pray to when seeking husbands: "St. Ann, St. Ann, send me a man." This is probably a good prayer for a prospective bride to invoke after she has booked the reception hall, a church, and a priest but has yet to line up a groom.

Some of the great saints were said to have the special gift of bilocation, even when they were alive. Being able to be in two places at the same time would certainly make a saint's work schedule more efficient, and St. Ann may be one of those bilocators. Jesus' grandmother has two shrines in the Archdiocese of New Orleans. The original shrine is on Ursulines Street, and it is a traditional cave-like grotto with a statue of St Ann in the center. Lots of artificial flowers and vigil lamps are presented at the shrine. There is a surprisingly large yard surrounding the grotto, with more statues and flowers. Pilgrims to the shrine sometimes pray the rosary while ascending the steps on their knees. There is no parish church there anymore; St. Ann's is now the big parish in Metairie, and it is also the National Shrine.

The shrines and the church dedicated to St. Ann are miles away from the church that honors her husband, St. Joachim. Does this make good sense? If the official Catholic Church wants to encourage the permanency of marriage, why do Sts. Ann and Joachim have separate churches? St. Joachim's church is on the West Bank, in the Barataria region, far away from his wife's church in Metairie on the east bank. What does this say about Jesus' grandparents?

Also popular in y'at Catholicism are novenas, devotions, and other prayers to Mary in her manifestation as Our Lady of Perpetual Help. This devotion is inspired by an ancient icon, a painting that depicts Mary holding the infant Jesus. Both have halos, and there are tiny angels on either side of Mary's face. Many churches had weekly devotions to Our Lady of Perpetual Help, which a supplicant could attend every week or for nine weeks as a novena. Replicas of the original painting hang in many older churches, and the devout and the desperate can be seen in silent prayer as they touch the picture with one hand. There are two suburban churches dedicated to Mary under this title, one in Belle Chasse on the West Bank and the other in Kenner near the Louis Armstrong International Airport. In fact, the Kenner church is the Catholic church closest to the airport, which is probably a good site for Our Lady of Perpetual Help.

The devotion to Our Lady of Perpetual Help has a strange and wonderful history. It is based on a painting. In the fourteenth or fifteenth centuries, a merchant from Crete saw the Byzantine-style painting on a wood backing. For unexplained reasons, the merchant did not buy the painting, but stole it from its owner. The merchant carried it to Rome where he later became mortally ill. As he lay dying, he called a friend to his deathbed and requested that the picture be hung in a church as restitution for his thievery. The merchant died, but his friend reneged on the promise. The friend's wife decided she wanted it for their home. But shortly thereafter, Mary appeared to the couple's young daughter and commanded that the picture be hung in a church. Mary revealed herself to the child as Holy Mary of Perpetual Help.

On March 27, 1499, the picture was solemnly enthroned on the high altar of St. Matthew's Church in Rome. For the next three hundred years, it was venerated and was the source of many miracles. In 1798 the French army, filled with the atheistic and anticlerical zeal of the French Revolution, seized Rome and leveled St. Matthew's Church. The portrait of Our Lady of Perpetual Help was rescued before the pillage took place and was held in security in different places for many years. Eventually Pope Pius IX declared that the Redemptorist order be given the painting, and they formally opened it to public view again in the church of St. Alfonso in Rome on April 26, 1866. The devotion to Our Lady of Perpetual Help spread again rapidly.

Devotion to St. Lucy, sometimes in the form of a personal novena, is done when a y'at has an eye disease or is losing vision. St. Lucy was a virgin martyr of the fourth century. The legend about her martyrdom is gruesome. She was said to be a wealthy Sicilian who was very generous to the poor. She refused offers of marriage, which enraged one suitor who falsely accused her of crimes. She was condemned to be violated in a brothel, but she was miraculously made immobile, and her virginity was preserved. She was then condemned to be burned to death, but that horrible torture did not work either. She eventually had her eyes plucked out and was killed with a sword. Modern-day problems with cataracts and near-sightedness are quite mild compared to Lucy's ordeal.

St. Peregrine, whose name comes from Latin words meaning to travel or to be a stranger, has developed a following among y'at Catholics as the "Cancer Saint." Personal novenas and other prayers are made to St. Peregrine to help someone afflicted with the disease. The story about Peregrine is that he was a member of the religious order of the Servants of Mary in thirteenth-century Italy. He developed cancer in his foot, which the doctors told him had to be amputated. He prayed all night not to lose his foot because, if he did, he would be unable to carry out his work of spreading the devotion to Mary as the Mother of God. In the morning, after Peregrine had been praying all night, the doctors arrived to amputate his foot, but the disease had vanished and his foot was healed. This miracle enhanced his reputation as a holy man, and many came to him for healing and were not disappointed.

Just as St. Peregrine is the "Cancer Saint," St. Alphonsus Liguori's help is prayed for as the "Arthritis Saint." The connection between Alphonsus and arthritis is unclear. It is also unclear whether y'ats have more rheumatism than other people and therefore need saintly help. Alphonsus started off as a successful lawyer in Naples in the eighteenth century. However, when he lost a big case because of a stupid mistake, he decided to give up the law and take up religion. Even a saint can be guilty of malpractice. He founded the Congregation of the Most Holy Redeemer, generally known as the Redemptorists. Father Seelos, New Orleans's newest saint, was a member of that order. There was a church dedicated to St. Alphonsus in the Irish Channel, even though he wasn't Irish, but the church was deconsecrated and turned into a cultural center. Another church, St. Mary's Assumption, is across the street. Father Seelos is buried in that church.

Y'ats also make novenas and have devotion for St. Roch. In fact, they have given his name to a broad, divided boulevard, St. Roch Avenue, which in turn gave the saint's name to the nearby neighborhood. Probably best known by people outside of the neighborhood is the seafood market that straddles the neutral ground of the divided street, the St. Roch Market. There is, however, no church dedicated to the saint, but there are two adjoining cemeteries in the St. Roch neighborhood dedicated to him. In one of those cemeteries is a tiny chapel that is marked to be the National Shrine of St. Roch. At one time it was popular among y'ats to seek cures from the saint and then festoon the walls and gates of the chapel with miniature artificial parts of the body that were healed by his intercession. Apparently the saint's healing record was pretty good because the chapel eventually ran out of room for displaying the devices.

St. Roch was a fourteenth-century holy man who contracted the plague while on a pilgrimage in Rome. The plague was almost always fatal in those days, but Roch survived through prayer while holed up in the woods being miraculously fed by a dog. He is usually pictured with the

St. Roch Seafood Market was named for the healing saint with the dog.

faithful dog at his side, and it has been reported that some people think the dog is at least as holy as Roch and offer prayers to the dog. It is too bad that the dog's name has not been passed down along with the rest of the saint's history. It would be fun to know that there was a St. Lassie or St. Snoopy. More important than his own cure, Roch cured others while he was alive. After he died, miracles of healing continued at his tomb.

It is easy to see how devotion to St. Roch would thrive in nineteenth-century New Orleans, which had its own recurring plagues of yellow fever and malaria. He is credited with protecting an entire congregation from yellow fever, not one fatality in an entire year, and the shrine and cemetery were erected to give thanks for his protection. The walled cemetery dedicated to St. Roch is unusual in that fourteen large statues depicting the stations of the cross are part of the burial site. The faithful gather there on Good Friday for the traditional journey along the Via Dolorosa.

In St. Mary's Church on Chartres Street is the National Shrine of St. Lazarus of Jerusalem. This saint is the eponymous patron of the Military and Hospital Order of the Knights of St. Lazarus of Jerusalem, a little-known international charitable organization that originally was made up of armed knights and crusaders. Membership is limited to those with deep pockets because the knights pledge to donate huge sums of money to fund the order's various charitable programs throughout the world, mainly in the Middle East. St. Lazarus was a personal friend of Jesus, who in his most dramatic miracle raised Lazarus from the dead three days after he had been buried. St. Lazarus is also identified as the beggar in Jesus' parable about the rich man and the beggar who died and were subjected to God's judgment. The knights consider both saints their patrons.

Two thousand years before there was Martha Stewart, there was St. Martha. St. Martha was one of Jesus' good friends who lived in Bethany. She was the sister of Mary Magdalene and the above-mentioned Lazarus. In the Gospel, Jesus takes issue with Martha after she scolds her sister for ignoring household chores and chatting with Jesus. In Luke's Gospel, Martha is described as being busy in the kitchen preparing dinner while Mary was with Jesus in the main room of their house. Jesus says that Mary was doing right because she was listening to his teachings. Nevertheless, Martha remained one of Jesus' closest friends, and the scriptures relate his visits and dinners with Martha, Mary, and Lazarus. There is a church dedicated to her in Harvey on the West Bank, and there are statues to St. Martha in several churches in New Orleans. Because she is the patron saint of all things having to do with the household and thus the patroness of gracious living, many y'ats pray for her direction and guidance, especially when planning a big dinner at home.

There is a popular devotion among y'at Catholic women to St. Gerard, the patron saint of expectant mothers. This patronage seems very odd for a man, especially one who was a celibate lay brother of the Redemptorist Order. In the early eighteenth century, Gerard Majella was born into poverty in Naples. His poor health kept him from his first career choice as a Capuchin monk, but St. Alphonsus, founder of the Redemptorists, reluctantly allowed him to join that order as a lay brother. Gerard became well-known for his sanctity and miracles. A desperate, distraught pregnant woman falsely accused Gerard of being her baby's father, and Gerard bore the accusation in silence. When the woman recanted her false testimony and cleared him, his role as a patron of expectant mothers began. He also gets invoked as patron of falsely accused people and, as an extension of his position as protector of pregnant women, the patron of the anti-abortion movement.

There is, coincidentally, another saint who is the patron of unborn children and expectant mothers, also a celibate male. In thirteenth-century Spain a man named Raymond joined an obscure religious order called the Mercedarians. He was known as Nonnatus, which in Latin literally means "not born." He was taken from his mother's womb in a gruesome form of caesarean section as she died in childbirth, and as a result some spiritual aura followed him. Like St. Gerard, he is invoked by expectant mothers and those falsely accused. Unlike St. Gerard, he seems to be virtually unknown in New Orleans. This is too bad; one of St. Raymond's accomplishments, for which he suffered torture, was crossing the Mediterranean Sea to ransom slaves from the Moors of Algiers. The Algiers connection should have made St. Raymond Nonnatus popular in the Crescent City, but nobody knows Nonnatus here.

Nearly every older church in the Archdiocese of New Orleans has a statue, usually near the main entrance door, of St. Anthony of Padua. For y'at Catholics, St. Anthony is a theological lost-and-found department. For reasons that are obscured by time and legend, St. Anthony, a thirteenth-century Franciscan friar and a contemporary of St. Francis of Assisi, developed a reputation hundreds of years later as the saint who could find lost stuff. In New Orleans churches, items that worshipers leave in the pews are placed at the statue of St. Anthony because the owners will know where to look for the lost articles after saying a quick prayer to the saint. Although St. Anthony has a good reputation and a respectable record of coming through when his help is sought in finding lost physical objects, he is of little help in regaining lost opportunities, lost sensibilities, lost minds, and lost innocence.

The 1938 Eucharistic Monstrance

One of the biggest events in the history of y'at Catholicism was the Eighth National Eucharistic Congress held in New Orleans October 17-20, 1938. The Municipal Auditorium and City Park were used to accommodate the large crowds of more than one hundred thousand people who participated. A special Eucharistic Congress emblem, altar, and bell were designed and constructed for the event.

The most spectacular device created for the Eucharistic Congress, by far, was a monstrance, the vessel in which the Eucharistic host is displayed.

To describe the 1938 monstrance is like reciting a passage from Homer's *The Iliad.* In *The Iliad,* Achilles, great hero of the Achaeans who are attacking the city of Troy, allows his dear friend Patroclus to wear his armor into battle while Achilles sulks in his tent. Patroclus is killed in battle, and the Trojans strip him of Achilles's magnificent armor. Hephaestus, the god of the forge and metalwork and friend of Achilles, fashions new armor for the hero. Homer spends many, many lines describing the intricate artistic detail embossed on the new shield. One wonders just how big that shield was to contain all that artwork and how long it took Hephaestus to create it. Similar intricate, exquisite artwork went into the creation of the 1938 Eucharistic Congress monstrance. The monstrance is enormous. Weighing twenty-four pounds, it stands forty-two inches from its base to the tip of a jeweled cross at the top. Gold, silver, and platinum were used by the artists to craft the monstrance, with 817 diamonds and 90 other jewels attached in various settings. The focal point to which an observer's eye is immediately drawn is the circular luna in the center, the glass-covered receptacle for the consecrated host. Out from the luna is a series of concentric circles, the nearest a ring of 231 diamonds. The next circle is a ring of fourteen enamel emblems depicting the national colors of the home countries of the clergy who served New Orleans from its earliest days. This colorful circle is supported by the hands of two silver angels, one on either side facing inward, with wings outstretched. Outward from the luna, the third circle of embossed gold looks like a parade but is actually a depiction of the First Eucharistic Congress in New Orleans in 1734. The artwork commemorates the procession of the Congress accompanying the Ursuline nuns to their new convent. Above that circle and under the jeweled cross are a chalice, a stole, and a missal, also in embossed gold. The final ring, also of brilliant gold, is composed of the symbols of the Eucharist, grapes and wheat. The rays of this ring point outward to give the appearance of a starburst. Just above the base, superimposed on part of the third and fourth rings, is the circular emblem of the 1938 Congress, for which the monstrance was crafted. Below the rings, at the top of the base, is a statuette in silver of the patroness of the archdiocese, Our Lady of Prompt Succor. There is also a small statue of St. Louis, King of France, patron saint of the archdiocese and Louisiana. Four additional statuettes represent the four types of clergy who served in the early days of the New Orleans church: diocesan, Franciscans, Vincentians, and Jesuits. On the base of the monstrance are the coats of arms of two popes, Pius VI, who established the diocese in 1793, and Pius IX , who was head of the church when New Orleans became an archdiocese in 1850. Completing the artwork of the base are the seals of the United States, Louisiana, and New Orleans; a set of shields of the archbishops and bishops who have served New Orleans; and another group of shields of the twenty-six dioceses carved from the original diocese of Louisiana and the Floridas. A photograph of the monstrance can be seen on page 69 of Charles E. Nolan's *A History of the Archdiocese of New Orleans.*

After the 1938 Eucharistic Congress was over, the magnificent monstrance was put into deep, secure storage and was not seen again for many years. In 1984, as part of the World's Fair in New Orleans, the Vatican Pavilion displayed many fine paintings and sculpture from museums in Vatican City. Displayed along with the splendid and marvelous works of Renaissance and modern art was the 1938 monstrance. It became the most popular item in the World Fair's collection. Y'ats could admire the grandiose beauty of Caravaggio's *The Deposition,* but they could identify more with the hometown-made elaborate monstrance. After the World's Fair closed, the monstrance was occasionally brought out for special devotions, often with an advance announcement that it would be used in benediction. During benediction, the procedure is for the priest to raise the monstrance containing the consecrated host and bless the congregation by making the sign of the cross with the heavy vessel. The twenty-four-pound 1938 monstrance may have thrown out a couple of priestly backs or possibly even threatened a sacerdotal hernia, but the majesty and solemnity of a benediction with the 1938 monstrance were well worth the physical risks.

The Vatican Pavilion

The 1984 World's Fair, officially named the 1984 Louisiana World Exhibition, was an exciting event in the history of the Crescent City. For six months, May to November, the riverfront site of the fair was filled with music, excitement, informative exhibits, good food, and entertainment. One of the most impressive exhibits of the exposition was the Vatican Pavilion at which was displayed a collection of works of art from the Vatican Museum and other museums and collections from Europe and the United States. The theme of the exhibit was "Jesus Christ Our Redeemer in Art: Images and Impact on Evangelization in the World Today." The exhibit was prepared through many months of work and fund raising by Dominican Father V.A. McInnes, an expert in art and the chairman of the Department of Judeo-Christian Studies at Tulane University. The exhibit allowed some spectacular paintings usually kept in the Vatican to be seen by y'at Catholics who would never get as far away from home as Rome, Georgia, let alone Rome, Italy. As soon as the fair began with an ominous eclipse of the sun darkening the sky just after the gates first opened, the word spread around the New Orleans area that there were some amazing sights to be seen in the Vatican Pavilion.

Indeed there were. In addition to the popular, local 1938 monstrance and *The Deposition,* there were El Greco's *Christ on the Cross;* a chasuble, the formal vestment worn by the priest at Mass, by Henri Matisse; Salvador Dali's strange, surreal *The Madonna of Port Lligat;* and many, many more. The word also spread that there was a huge painting by Michelangelo. Everybody had heard of Michelangelo, and this was the one opportunity to see a masterpiece by one of history's greatest artists up close. Sure enough, there was a huge painting taking up the entire wall of one gallery. Alost ten feet by six and a half feet, *The Deposition,* a dramatic and moving depiction of Jesus' body being laid on a slab to prepare it for burial, was the largest and most powerful of the paintings in the pavilion. And sure enough, there was the artist's name on the sign next to the painting, Michelangelo Caravaggio. But the word began to spread that he wasn't the real Michelangelo, the guy who created *David* and painted the ceiling of the Sistine Chapel. Some people were disappointed. They did not realize that in Renaissance Italy there was more than one great artist with the first name of Michelangelo. Patient docents at the pavilion explained over and over that the real Michelangelo, he of the Sistine Chapel fame, had the family name of Buonarotti. To make the situation more frustrating and confusing, a marble statue of *Christ Resurrected* appeared in the brochure and guide books printed before the fair opened. That statue was the work of the "real" Michelangelo, but at the last minute the Vatican Museum refused to include it in the artworks shipped to New Orleans. A huge tapestry by Raphael was substituted, and it took up an entire wall in one of the galleries. The entire scene of the Resurrection was portrayed on it, not just the figure of Christ, so the visitors got more than they expected.

Before visitors to the Vatican Pavilion could see *The Deposition,* the 1938 Monstrance, and all the other great art, they had to pass the very first exhibit in the first gallery. There stood in dark bronze, seven feet tall, right arm extended and hand beckoning, a statue by French sculptor Auguste Rodin of John the Baptist, patron saint of Jean-Baptiste Le Moyne, Sieur de Bienville, founder of the city of New Orleans. The huge sculpture stopped visitors in their tracks. The great saint was naked. Naked as a jaybird. Naked as the day he was born. In his birthday suit. Full-frontal nudity. Anatomically correct. Buck naked. How does a parent explain to an impressionable youngster what a seven-foot-tall statue of a naked man waving his hand is doing in a building sponsored by the Catholic Church? A good y'at parent might have engaged the child as follows:

"Mama, look; the man's naked! Ooh!"

"Uhh, yeah, dawlin'. That's John the Baptist. It's just a statue."

"How come he's not wearing any clothes? You can see his privates."

"Look, this is art, OK? It ain't like it's dirty pictures or nothin'. Now let's go see something else."

John the Baptist's statue provided a good lesson in great art—and good explanations—for all who gazed upon it.

Manresa

The word "Manresa" means only one thing to y'at Catholics. It is the Jesuit retreat house for men, an hour's drive upriver on the River Road in Convent, Louisiana. A Manresa retreat is part of being male and Catholic in New Orleans. In buildings that date from the 1840s, the Jesuit fathers conduct weekly retreats for up to one hundred and twenty men. The formula has changed little if at all from the first retreats held there in 1931. Three days of prayer, Mass, silence, meditation, and a series of instructions by a retreat master based on the five-hundred-year-old *Spiritual Exercises of St. Ignatius Loyola*. Y'ats are only vaguely aware that Manresa is the place in the Catalonia region of Spain where Ignatius drafted his *Spiritual Exercises* while recuperating from a leg wound suffered in a battle. To a y'at, Manresa is a recurring ritual in the rhythm of the year, just like the opening day of shrimp season or Thanksgiving or the first home game of the New Orleans Saints. Groups of men go together to Manresa every year, year after year, in an experience that is part male-bonding, part getting away from the stress of daily life, and all spiritual. Manresa is muscular, vigorous, masculine Catholicism, an annual spirituality training camp. Attendees can hike or jog on the levee and sweat while meditating. Manresa is where a man, dressed in flip-flop shower shoes and a T-shirt that advertises Harley-Davidson motorcycles, can pray the rosary, loudly, with a hundred other men. Manresa is an opportunity to sit quietly in an outdoor easy chair in a lane of ancient live oaks dripping with Spanish moss, read a book, smoke a cigar without someone complaining about the smell, and listen for the deep pulses of life. The rooms are spare but cheerful; the boarding-house-style meals are plentiful and hearty. Statues and pictures of saints and the Blessed Mother are everywhere. There are old-fashioned devotions, the rosary, and the stations of the cross. There are several tiny chapels for intense personal prayer. Like monasteries of old, bells signal the events of the day, calling the silent men to prayer and instruction. The experience was succinctly described by the late New Orleans Judge Louis Yarrut, a Jew who regularly made retreats at Manresa: "It is a place where nobody speaks to anyone, and everyone speaks to God."

The Pope's Visit

Perhaps the largest celebration in the history of y'at Catholicism was the visit to New Orleans by Pope John Paul II in September 1987. More than a year of planning and a lot of money went into the event. Some streets were resurfaced, and new palm trees were planted on Carrollton Avenue, along which the pope rode to the archbishop's residence. On Saturday morning, the pope held an audience in the Louisiana Superdome for young people where he heard local music and dispensed some cheerful papal advice and guidance. The pontiff's presence in the Superdome had near-miraculous effects beginning the next day. The New Orleans Saints played a game on Sunday afternoon in that same arena, and they won handily. As one of the television announcers remarked as the Saints kept scoring, there was no way that the Saints could lose in a place that was blessed by the pope's presence the day before. For the first time in their twenty-year history, the Saints went on to a have a winning season that year.

The biggest event of John Paul II's visit was the open-air Mass in a large field near the lakefront on the campus of the University of New Orleans. Tickets were free and distributed through the church parishes. Attendees were told to park far away and take shuttles. Over two hundred thousand people were expected. Concession stands and portable toilets were set up, and medical shelters were erected. Police, firefighters, and Secret Service agents drew up contingency and emergency plans. But it was early September in New Orleans, and the summer heat had not yet slacked. Someone in the archdiocese's planning department admitted to the news media that deaths at the Mass were expected, as many as half a dozen due to the expected heat and the fact that many attending would be elderly or infirm. Death at the pope's Mass! The fear and drama were too much for many y'ats. They decided to stay home and watch the solemnities on television, with their air conditioners running.

The Mass was scheduled for late afternoon, and the faithful were urged to arrive hours before to ease the crush. As the afternoon wore on under the blazing sun, lots of y'ats showed up, although not as many as expected. Mass with the pope should be a formal event, but with the sun bright and the temperature above 90 degrees, many y'ats showed up dressed for the beach or Jazz Fest. Lots of straw hats and Thermos jugs of cold drinks were carried to Mass along with cameras and sunscreen. The weather forecasters predicted a 50 percent chance of an afternoon thundershower, a fairly common prediction for a summer afternoon in south Louisiana. By mid-afternoon, the meteorologists' forecasts appeared accurate. Dark, heavy clouds began to build, and flashes of lightning were followed by rolling thunder. First the big drops hit, then the torrent. It was a summer afternoon in New Orleans, and Mother Nature did not give a hoot that the pope was scheduled to say Mass outdoors.

About an hour before the Holy Father was to arrive, the skies started dumping tons of water on the area. This meteorological event revealed a cultural trait common to y'ats, a reluctance if not refusal to use rain gear. Despite the fact that a y'at doesn't need a weatherman to tell him that there is a good chance of thunderstorms on any given summer afternoon, the ever-optimistic y'at believes that the 50 percent chance of no thunderstorms applies to wherever he may be that afternoon. So it came to pass that, while waiting for the pope, thousands of y'ats got drenched, soaked to the skin. It was not just the local people who got wet. Dozens of well-dressed—and sweating— Secret Service agents, electronic monitors in their ears and clutching purses and concealed shoulder holsters, also got wet. Some of them had small umbrellas, and a few had raincoats, but the summer deluge doused them anyway. Soaked and dripping, y'ats and Secret Service agents, nuns and priests milled around looking miserable and foolish as the rain poured.

Then a wave of murmur spread the news that the pope had arrived. All stretched their necks and stood on their folding chairs to get a glimpse of the man for whom they had waited—and gotten soaking wet—for so many hours. Just as the Popemobile, as the pope's bullet-proof car came to be known, entered the grounds, the rain stopped and the clouds thinned. A big-budget movie production could not have staged it any better. John Paul II smiled, laughed, waved, and blessed the crowds as the Popemobile ran through the ruts and puddles of rainwater. Mass was ready to start.

After any hard summer thunderstorm, the temperature drops. So instead of heat exhaustion and sunstroke felling the vulnerable, the problem for the medical personnel became hypothermia and dangerous chills. Stretcher bearers began carrying wet, shaking victims with blue lips to ambulances. No hypothermia deaths occurred, but the preparations for treating heat stroke were unnecessary. Thousands stood wet and shivering as the pope began in his heavy but pleasantly accented English, "In the name of the Father. . . ."

The Mass was elegant and beautiful. The prayers of the faithful were offered in several languages, including English, French, Spanish, Swahili, Vietnamese, and Choctaw. New Orleans's well known jazz clarinetist, Pete Fountain, played the old spiritual "Just a Closer Walk With Thee" more sweetly than he had ever done before. The rain was over; cheer and happiness returned.

As the Holy Father distributed Communion to thousands, with the help of a large group of priests and Eucharistic ministers, a rain-generated phenomenon took place. Hundreds of devout women approached His Holiness in garments that would most likely have caused consternation and would have resulted in them being asked to leave an ordinary church on an ordinary Sunday. But Mass outside in the rain with the pope is anything but ordinary. The women looked as though they were participants in some wet tee-shirt contest. Imagine the Holy Father reaching out to give the consecrated bread, the body and blood of Jesus, to someone whose wet skivvies and more are showing through her wet shirt. As Karol Wojtela, John Paul II had been harassed, humiliated, and tortured by the Nazis and the Communists. He had seen all sorts of sordid and terrible sights. He did not bat an eye at distributing the Eucharist to women in wet tee shirts.

The pope's visit was an event of wonder, the greatest moment in the history of New Orleans Catholicism. The city made a permanent memorial of the event by officially designating the closed-off block of Chartres Street in front of St. Louis Cathedral Place Jean-Paul Deux. Jean-Paul Deux, or John Paul II, charmed everyone with his warm and cheerful remarks. His command of English, though excellent, did not include idiomatic regional expressions. That's too bad. It would have been a truly great moment in the history of the Catholic Church had the archbishop or one of the pope's advisers coached him so that he could have begun Mass with the New Orleans salutation, "Where y'at!" To which the faithful would have responded thunderously, "Awright!" It was indeed all right.

CHAPTER 7

Following the Liturgical Calendar

Advent and Christmas

The Church calendar begins with the first Sunday in Advent, usually the Sunday following Thanksgiving. The beginning of Advent, the period before Christmas in which the prayers and scripture readings at Mass prepare for the coming birth of Jesus, coincides in New Orleans with the annual opening of a dazzling and spectacular light display in City Park. Hundreds of thousands, maybe millions, of lights are set in arrays and light sculptures along a series of streets in the park. Multicolored stars hang from live oak trees, and the park's rose garden twinkles with tiny lights too numerous to count. There are winter scenes, idealized scenes of rural life, animals, birds, and oh, yes Christmas themes. When this display, which is sponsored by City Park and a number of local businesses, was first presented, it was called Christmas in the Oaks. The display lasts the full Advent and Christmas seasons from Thanksgiving until the weekend following New Year's Day. After a few years, Christmas in the Oaks became bigger and more elaborate. The miniature train, something usually operating only during the day for children's rides, was decorated in hundreds of tiny lights, and nighttime rides attracted adults as well. Visitors could take the tour in open mule-drawn carriages. There was music in the air. Weddings were held amidst all the lights. Perhaps the use of the word "Christmas" seemed exclusionary for non-Christians, especially those whose generosity made the display so enjoyable. The people in charge of Christmas in the Oaks decided that, because it was more than just a celebration of the birth of Jesus, they would change the name of the event to Celebration in the Oaks. The event has had that official designation ever since.

Y'ats are slow to adapt to name changes. Most y'at Catholics believe in the slogan "Keep Christ in Christmas." Although they didn't really object to the name change, with traditional y'at nonchalance, they tended to ignore it. Y'ats will go for a drive though City Park around Christmastime, and no matter what the official name of the display is, they call it "Christmas in the Oaks."

A y'at Christmas is not very different from Christmas celebrations elsewhere in the Deep South. They may attend midnight Mass wearing a nice new sweater, even though the air conditioner has to be turned on in the church. They observe Christmas with trees and turkey dinner with oyster dressing. There is, however, at least one practice of Christmas observance that is unique to New Orleans. As with virtually every other celebration in New Orleans, sacred or profane, food is the focus. In the nineteenth century, long before evening Masses were authorized on Christmas Eve, when the church rules required that anyone who wanted to receive Holy Communion at Mass had to be fasting completely from the preceding midnight, Christmas midnight Mass was a big event indeed. Because the rule said "fasting from midnight" and Mass started at midnight, revelers could eat and drink at parties practically up to Mass time. Midnight Mass was usually what was then designated a solemn High Mass, meaning there was a lot of singing and incense and it lasted well into the early morning hours. By the time midnight Mass was over, y'ats were hungry again. There was no need to go to bed hungry, just to wake up and prepare a big Christmas dinner during the day. For the nineteenth-century French-Creole Catholics, forerunners of today's y'at Catholics, midnight Mass and eating were always a family event, with big, extended families taking part. The early morning feast following midnight Mass came to be called réveillon, which derives from the French verb *réveiller*, meaning to wake up. (The English military term "reveille" is of the same origin.) Réveillon was a feast indeed. It usually included daube glacé, which is jellied beef brisket seasoned with bay leaf, cloves, and pepper; raw oysters; pastries filled with jelly and laced with brandy and liqueurs; eggnog; and champagne. There was often for dessert a Bûche de Noël, a cake in the shape of a yule log. By the time réveillon was over, the dawn of Christmas Day had arrived, and the family could go sleep it off after a hearty round of *Joyeux Noël* to everyone.

The celebration of Christmas with a family réveillon at home slowly died out, especially after the church rules on times of Mass and fasting before Holy Communion were relaxed. Many y'ats attend Mass on Christmas Eve in the late afternoon. Some churches no longer schedule midnight Mass as attendance dwindled because of other options. However, many New Orleans restaurants have revived the name, if not the specifics, by developing special menus to be served during the Christmas season. A family can go to a fine restaurant in the evening during the holidays and enjoy a réveillon dinner without having to wait until two o'clock in the morning on Christmas. Besides, there aren't any dishes to clean.

Epiphany

Following Christmas, the next important date on the calendar of y'at Catholicism is the Feast of the Epiphany. From time immemorial, this celebration was held on January 6, and it marks the end of the Christmas season. In the British tradition, it is known as Twelfth Night. The "Twelve Days of Christmas," celebrated in the song with partridges in pear trees, runs from Christmas to the Epiphany. Y'ats once called the day "Little Christmas" (pronounced *LIL CRIS-mus*) because children received their gifts then, just as the baby Jesus received his gifts from the three wise men. However, as a result of Vatican II, the church hierarchy, without consulting the devout y'at Catholic on the street, changed the Feast of the Epiphany from its traditional date of January 6 to the Sunday following New Year's Day. Y'ats paid little attention to the change. *Everyone* in New Orleans knows that January 6 is the Epiphany, even if they don't know what the word means. For the record, "epiphany" means a sudden revelation or realization of the importance of an event. In Christian theology, it means the revelation of Jesus to the gentiles, the three men who came from the East guided by a star.

These three men are people of legend as well as being mentioned in the Gospels. They are sometimes called the three wise men, astrologers, or the Magi. The three visitors from the East who brought gold, frankincense, and myrrh to Jesus have been identified in tradition as Balthazar, Melchior, and Gaspar. Y'ats know them as the three kings, a royal title also found in the Christmas carol, "We Three

Kings of Orient Are." The identification of the Magi as the three kings is very significant to New Orleans Catholicism because January 6, Twelfth Night, Little Christmas, or the Epiphany, marks the beginning of the most important time of the year. Christmas is over; it's time to start thinking about Mardi Gras.

The physical, cultural, spiritual, and religious bridge between Christmas and Mardi Gras is, as one might expect in New Orleans, food. The specific food is king cake. It is so called because the pastry is served for the first time on January 6, the day the three kings visited Jesus. In recent years, driven by commercial demand, local bakeries are baking king cakes before January 6. Y'ats who are true believers will not, however, eat king cake before January 6. Who knows, it might even be a venial sin.

Purchasing and eating king cake is much more than consuming a sweet dessert. It is ceremony, it is tradition, it is celebration, it is one of the deepest rhythms in the y'at psyche. You must first decide where to buy your king cake. Beginning around January 6, there is frequent debate throughout the city of New Orleans over the endless, never-resolved question: Who makes the best king cake? This question cannot be answered because it is hardly possible to compare a traditional, brioche-style king cake to one that has been filled with cream cheese and gooey blueberry filing. Some purists believe that Randazzo's Goodchildren Bakery, originally in Chalmette, bakes the finest king cakes; other y'ats insist that Haydel's on Jefferson Highway can't be beaten; and there are y'ats who wistfully remember McKenzie's Bakery, whose king cakes maybe were not the best but were the most traditional. The debate has become an integral part of the observance of the Feast of the Epiphany.

Also integral to the feast day are the suspense and mystery of the imbedded plastic baby and the anxiety of discovery. Every king cake comes with a baby to be inserted before serving. It represents Jesus, the baby whom the three kings honored with royal gifts. In New Orleans parlance, it is always called "the baby." The king cake is the focus of a group ceremony—at school, at the office, at a picnic, at home. The person slicing the cake is careful to feel for the baby and moves the knife away if the baby is nicked. This is not because the king-cake slicer thinks that it is sacrilegious to stick a knife into an image of the Christ child; rather, it is because the rule of king-cake consumption is that the person who finds the baby has to buy the next cake. It is ironic that a ceremony that celebrates the joy of gift giving is subject to much scrutiny by stingy people who like to eat king cake that somebody else has bought, but don't like to buy it themselves. Alas, y'ats are human, too, and sometimes cheat for a slice of king cake. King-cake parties are usually held weekly, beginning January 6, with the person in the group who got the baby providing the cake for the next party. The last king cakes are eaten on Mardi Gras. There are people who eat king cake in Lent, but they are not authentic y'ats. Eating king cake in Lent is at least a venial sin.

Celebration of the Feast of the Epiphany takes place not just in churches and in schools and businesses where king cakes are eaten. To mark the beginning of the Mardi Gras season, an organization calling themselves the Phunny Phorty Phellows hires a streetcar for the evening of January 6, stocks it with king cakes and champagne, and sets off along the St. Charles Avenue streetcar line for an evening of noisy fun. It can probably be said with assurance that no one on that streetcar discusses the theological significance of the day, the revelation of Jesus to the gentiles. While the Phunny Phorty Phellows are riding the streetcar Uptown, a very old Carnival organization is having its masked ball downtown. For more than 125 years, the Twelfth Night Revelers have opened the Mardi Gras season with an elegant ball. They, too, have a king cake. Part of the Revelers' tableau at their ball is for several masked men costumed as chefs and bakers to bring a large cake into the middle of the ballroom floor. Colored ribbons spread out from under the cake, and the *jeunes filles,* the debutantes who are presented that night, each take hold of a ribbon. On signal, they pull the ribbons, and the ends hidden under the cake appear. Some have silver beans attached, but the girl who gets the gold bean is declared the queen of the ball. Then the ladies in their white dresses perform one of the trickiest duties of a debutante: eating king cake while wearing an expensive white dress and long white gloves. All done in the spirit of honoring the three kings who brought gifts to Jesus.

On the liturgical calendar, the Feast of the Epiphany is the closing date of the Christmas season and the beginning of Ordinary Time. There is nothing ordinary about the y'at celebrations that follow January 6. The beginning of Ordinary Time can create either a hectic or a leisurely mood among y'ats. Those who dismiss astrology as superstition should be aware of the powerful effect of the moon on the lives, fortunes, and moods of everyone in the city of New Orleans. Easter is the first Sunday following the first full moon after the vernal equinox, so the date of Mardi Gras varies from year to year and can be anywhere from the first week of February to the first week of March. The church tradition begins the penitential season of Lent on Ash Wednesday, forty days before Easter. Actually, Ash Wednesday is not forty calendar days before Easter. The forty days are only the weekdays; Sundays are not included. The day before Ash Wednesday is, of course, Fat Tuesday, or Mardi Gras, the day on which the Carnival season that began on January 6 comes to a tumultuous end. The same amount of celebration and partying will take place between January 6 and Mardi Gras without regard to the duration of the season. Whether the season is one month or two, parades will roll, costumes will be worn, and king cake will be eaten. The only difference is that, in a longer season, more king cake gets consumed.

St. Blaise and the Candles

On February 2, while the rest of the country observes Groundhog Day, the Catholic Church quietly observes one of the most ancient rituals in Christianity, the Day of Candlemas. This date has pagan origins. In the Celtic Wiccan tradition, February 2 is a cross-quarter day, halfway between the winter solstice and the vernal equinox. The ancients called it Imbolc and celebrated it as a fertility ritual. The modern image of the groundhog coming out of the hole in the ground to check on the sun is a modern manifestation. Perhaps the blessing of the candles was a Christian twist on this ancient observance. On Candlemas, the candles that will be used at Mass during the following year are blessed in a solemn ceremony. Although Candlemas is not a well-observed event in y'at Catholicism, its significance is manifested the next day on the Feast of St. Blaise.

Long, long before Dr. Heimlich invented his famous procedure for assisting someone who is choking, Christians invoked the protection of St. Blaise. In the early fourth century, Blaise was a bishop in the town of Sebaste in

Armenia. The Roman emperors were still chasing Christians then, and to avoid persecution Blaise hid in a cave. Local farmers and herders brought their sick and wounded animals to him, and he blessed and cured them. One day a mother brought her young son to Blaise because the boy was choking on a fish bone stuck in his throat. Blaise healed the boy, and his reputation as a wonder worker spread. The Roman authorities eventually caught him and put him in prison. The grateful mother brought food and candles to Blaise while he was in jail. He was later executed as a martyr to the Christian faith. However, a practice began that is still conducted on his feast day, February 3. The faithful go before a priest, deacon, or lay minister, who then hold two crossed, unlighted candles, blessed the day before at Candlemas, under the person's chin near the neck, and a blessing is given. This blessing is believed to help prevent choking on foreign objects and to ward off illnesses of the throat.

One of the greatest assists in New Orleans to St. Blaise's blessing is the electric filet knife. Once upon a time y'ats ate a lot of fish with bones. Whole fried fish were eaten not just at home but in many restaurants. Even filets of fish often included the fine rib bones that were very difficult to remove with the old-fashioned butcher knives and other knives that were used to filet fish. The city's folklore was once rife with stories of how someone—usually the victim's identity was vague or unknown—had choked horribly on a fish bone and had to be rushed to Charity Hospital for emergency surgery. Many people were afraid to eat fish unless there was some sort of certification by the chef that there were no bones in the filet. The most dangerous fish seems to have been the croaker, a fish rarely seen on restaurant menus anymore. It is a close relative of the redfish but does not grow as large. Therein lies the danger. The croaker was usually served fried and whole, and no meal of whole, fried croaker could begin without a discussion of the dangers involved, a warning about choking, and the strong belief that the croaker contained more bones than did other fish. It was accepted as a scientific fact that a croaker had more bones. There was no room in this discussion of fish bones for any scientific skepticism, no questioning the faith-based fact that a croaker was bonier than any other fish that swam in lake or bayou.

Then the electric filet knife was invented, and quickly fishermen and fish-market butchers could not only easily cut the filet from the backbone, they could deftly remove the rib bones with only a minimal loss of fish flesh. Boneless fish became the standard fare everywhere, and whole, fried croakers disappeared from restaurant menus.

Did prayers to St. Blaise result in the invention of the electric filet knife? Was Dr. Heimlich under the great saint's protection when he devised his diaphragm-popping maneuver to dislodge a foreign object in a victim's throat? Maybe these questions are yet more Mysteries of the Faith. What is fact is that y'ats are eating fish that are not only without bones but without fear of bones. Stories of some y'at choking on fish bones and being rushed to Charity Hospital have disappeared from the urban folklore. St. Blaise seems to have heard the prayers.

Mardi Gras

It is utterly impossible to overemphasize the influence of Mardi Gras on the culture of New Orleans. Although pre-Lenten festivals are held many places in the world, in New Orleans the day has become the benchmark for everything.

Time is reckoned and life exists either before or after Mardi Gras. Social, business, and educational events must yield to the inexorable cultural pressure of the season that starts on January 6 and ends at midnight as Ash Wednesday begins.

Much has been written about Mardi Gras, some of which is actually true. Many stories focus on the public events, the parades, and the costumes in the street. Other books talk about the behind-the-scenes preparations for parades and Carnival balls. Most brush lightly over the fact that Mardi Gras is a Catholic celebration.

Mardi Gras, as is generally known, is French for Fat Tuesday. The Tuesday before Ash Wednesday is "fat" because it is the last day before the penitential observances of Lent begin, with the rule against eating any kind of meat on Ash Wednesday and on the Fridays in Lent. Ash Wednesday and Good Friday are also days of fasting, on which faithful Catholics avoid eating between the two light meals and the one full meal allowed. On the other days in Lent, Catholics are urged to fast and to abstain from meat as well, although that practice is personal. To prepare for all this somber penance and mortification of the flesh in order to cleanse the soul, long ago began the tradition of a rousing and raucous party. The basic idea is not very different from the Second Law of Thermodynamics, which says that heat always flows from a higher temperature to a lower temperature. By partying at a high energy before Lent begins, so goes the comparison, there is a better flow—and hence penitence when the somber, low-energy day of Ash Wednesday arrives. Who can be contrite on Ash Wednesday if the preceding weeks have been dreary and monotonous?

Synonymous in the y'at idiom with Mardi Gras is the term "carnival." Although "carnival" has come to mean a fair or a circus in places away from New Orleans, y'at usage is closer to the original Latin roots. *Carne* is meat or flesh in Latin. The word shows up on menus in Mexican and Latin restaurant that serve carne asada, a form of roast beef. The last syllable of carnival comes from the Latin word for good-bye, *vale*. On the day before Ash Wednesday, the revelers are saying good-bye to meat, because, if they are observant they will eat little meat before Easter. The farewell to meat is the basis for the traditional float of Le Boeuf Gras, the Fatted Cow, near the beginning of the Rex parade on Mardi Gras morning. The Fatted Cow symbolizes what once was an actual event: A cow or steer was butchered and roasted whole so that revelers could eat so much meat that they would not want any for the next six weeks, making their fasting easier.

The term Shrove Tuesday is sometimes used far away from New Orleans to name the day before Ash Wednesday; it is never used by y'ats. Shrove Tuesday identifies the day as the third and last day of Shrovetide, an old observance that made the Sunday, Monday, and Tuesday before Lent days of penance, too. This practice never made it to New Orleans. The idea that those three days are supposed to be a period of penitential observance is utterly at odds with y'at tradition.

Although Mardi Gras and New Orleans have become identified with each other, Mardi Gras was observed along the Mississippi River many years before New Orleans was founded. In fact, the first Mass ever celebrated in Louisiana was on Mardi Gras on February 27, 1699. The explorer Pierre Le Moyne, Sieur d'Iberville, Bienville's older brother, moored his ship at a landing downriver from the site that would be chosen for the city of New Orleans. Iberville named the spot Pointe du Mardi Gras and the nearby small waterway Bayou Mardi Gras. Iberville's records show that Mass was celebrated that day, but the reports do not, however, mention throwing and wearing beads, noisy parades, and too much beer. Louisiana's first Mardi Gras set the religious tone of the day with a Mass.

Mass and Mardi Gras still go together. The Krewe of Endymion, the largest Carnival club with more than two thousand members and dozens of huge floats, holds its immensely popular parade and Extravaganza on the Saturday night before Mardi Gras. For the members, the event is as much endurance test as it is fun. The members meet at the Louisiana Superdome about midday to eat, drink, don their costumes, and get transported to City Park to board the floats at the beginning of the parade. The parade starts around 4:30, and it takes several hours before the last float reaches the Superdome for the all-night music, dancing, eating, and drinking. Those who are still functioning at four in the morning on Sunday are not thinking about going to Mass that morning; they don't have to. In a tradition that is part of the festivities, a priest-member offers Mass in the Superdome on Saturday after-noon, before the devout krewe members have imbibed too freely. When he concludes with, "Go in peace to love and to serve the Lord," the Endymion maskers are ready to get aboard their floats and show their love for the crowds by showering them with several tons of beads. Where else do people spend huge amounts of money to entertain public crowds with parades at which huge amounts of beads, dolls, and trinkets are given away to strangers? Surely this is in keeping with the message of Jesus to love one another.

One of the theories of the origins of Mardi Gras is that it is a Christian spin-off of the Roman festival of the Lupercalia. Some of the rituals observed by the pagan Romans are rather strange, but some of the rituals observed by modern Christians at Mardi Gras are just as strange. There are also similarities. The Lupercalia was celebrated in February in ancient Rome. It seems to have begun much earlier in preliterate times as a fertility rite involving wolves. The Lupercalia was conducted by a body of priests called the Luperci. The priests slaughtered goats and dogs as a sacrifice to the gods. Two of the young Luperci then received a mark of blood on their foreheads with the bloody knives. The blood was then wiped away with a woolen cloth dipped in milk. This ritual may be a vestige of the legend that Romulus and Remus, the mythical founders of Rome, were orphaned as infants and raised by a mother wolf who nursed them with her milk. The name Lupercalia is derived from the Latin word for wolf, *lupus.* The next steps in the Lupercalia ceremony were odd indeed. After the blood was wiped away, the two young Luperci were required to laugh aloud. A great feast followed at which the sacrificed animals were consumed. After the meal, all the Luperci picked up leather thongs made from the hides of the sacrificed animals. They then divided into two groups and ran around the Palantine Hill in Rome striking with their thong-whips any woman who came near. It was believed that a blow from one of the Luperci's whips would render a woman fertile.

The pagan Roman and Greek gods are an integral part of Mardi Gras. Many of the Carnival parades are staged by krewes with names of classical deities such as Proteus, Saturn, Orpheus, and Iris. Because of Mardi Gras, an authentic y'at knows as much about the ancient gods of Greece and Rome as he knows about Catholic theology. One of the biggest and most popular parades is the Krewe of Bacchus, named for the Roman god of wine. The parade usually begins at 5 p.m. on the Sunday before Mardi Gras. Like all parades, there is a lot of preparation and planning.

Many hours before the parade, the floats are towed to the marshal area, which is near the corner of Magazine Street and Napoleon Avenue. Nearby is St. Henry's Catholic Church, whose pastor, Monsignor Henry Englebrecht, is a joyous y'at. Father Henry invites friends and parishioners to his rectory for an all-day Bacchus party that starts around noon and goes until the last Bacchus float disappears into the night. The early popes and the church fathers of antiquity must squirm in their holy graves as they behold the joyful spectacle of a Catholic priest in good standing throwing a party in honor of a pagan god. These ancient holy men dedicated their lives to writing, preaching, and teaching that the pagan gods of the ancient world must not be honored.

The visual media have focused on the bawdy, raunchy activities on Bourbon Street to show Mardi Gras to the world outside New Orleans. The neighborhood marching clubs like the Jefferson City Buzzards, well over one hundred years old; the Skull and Bones marching groups of the Tremé neighborhood; and the hundreds of decorated flatbed truck floats that follow the Rex parade are seldom shown. These vital elements of Mardi Gras have been a part of Carnival for generations. In even further contrast to the raunchiness of the Bourbon Street revelers are the society Carnival balls in which older gentlemen in white tie and tails present young women in white gowns and white gloves to a dressed-to-the-teeth crowd in a pure display of elegance. Farewell to meat is stated in style.

Mardi Gras is the manifestation of Catholicism at its basic, emotional level. It is a pure and primitive form of religiosity, unadulterated by the rationalist influences of the Age of Enlightenment or the tangential effects of Calvinist gloom. In Mardi Gras, y'at Catholicism retains the sensual spirit of the pre-Reformation Mediterranean world salted with Afro- Caribbean passion, removed from Nordic seriousness and Protestant sensibilities.

Ash Wednesday

"Teach us to care and not to care. Teach us to sit still." So wrote T.S. Eliot in his poem "Ash Wednesday." Eliot was born and lived in St. Louis, Missouri, before moving to Britain and becoming one of the most famous English poets of the twentieth century, and there is no evidence that he ever participated in New Orleans Mardi Gras. Yet his words for the solemn day after Mardi Gras are fitting for the occasion. New Orleans has long used the phrase the "City That Care Forgot" to identify itself as a place of pleasure and parties. But on Ash Wednesday, y'ats do remember to care for their city as they watch the clean-up crews haul away the hundreds of tons of trash and garbage that covered the streets of the parades routes for the preceding several days. The filth and chaos of all that trash is a strong reminder that life is short and unpredictable. These strong visual incentives send y'ats to churches in droves on Ash Wednesday.

The beads of Tuesday are no more. An authentic y'at never wear beads on Ash Wednesday or during Lent, even if the y'at's guests are loaded down with them as they are dropped off at the airport. A y'at probably considers wearing Mardi Gras beads on Ash Wednesday a form of venial sin. One of the solemn practices of Ash Wednesday is to pack all the beads acquired during the parade season into bags and boxes and take them to the attic. One of the theories about the cause of New Orleans houses settling into the foundation dirt is that the attics keep filling up with beads, and the weight is too much for the soft mud on which the houses stand.

Priests who come to New Orleans from far away and are not yet acculturated in Mardi Gras and y'at Catholicism stand in awe at the extent of participation and intensity of devotion on Ash Wednesday. In places like Cleveland, Poughkeepsie, and Minneapolis, Ash Wednesday is just another, cold dreary day in winter. Going to church for ashes is not a high priority. But in New Orleans, the churches are packed. People who are not regular in their attendance of Sunday Mass line up for the mark of the ashes on their foreheads, and y'ats do not wipe the ashes off. The symbol is publicly displayed. Even local television announcers may appear on the evening news still showing the mark of mortality. Many non-Catholics feel the powerful symbolism in the ceremony, and they, too, line up for ashes. Ash Wednesday's popularity and intensity are a direct result of Mardi Gras. Mardi Gras exists because of Ash Wednesday.

St. Patrick's Day

Mardi Gras is barely over and Lent barely begun when the aftershocks of the Carnival season begin. The first of these is St. Patrick's Day. Depending on the date of Mardi Gras, St. Patrick's Day, March 17, can be very soon after Ash Wednesday. Ash Wednesday can be as late at the first week of March, which means that celebrations honoring the patron saint of Ireland can sometimes begin almost as soon as all the Mardi Gras trash has been collected. The focus of the celebrations is in a neighborhood that is as much myth as it is geography, the Irish Channel. The neighborhood, bounded roughly by Magazine Street, St. Joseph Street,

Jackson Avenue, and the Mississippi River, was settled in the 1830s by the first large influx of Irish immigrants. It was also a place where German and, later, Sicilian immigrants settled. These newcomers were all mostly unskilled laborers, economic refugees from intractable poverty and worse in Europe. Thousands of Irish arrived in the mid-nineteenth century to escape the potato famine in Ireland. Poor, illiterate, and unskilled, they took the dirtiest and most dangerous job available, digging the New Basin Canal. Several thousand Irishmen died digging that canal, a place of collapsing mud walls, malaria, and yellow fever.

No Irish families have lived in the Irish Channel for many years, but the nostalgia for the past that never was and the mythical and romantic notions of what being Irish means and who St. Patrick was color all perceptions. In truth and fact, in New Orleans, St. Patrick's Day is a second round of parades, a means of helping those suffering from Mardi Gras withdrawal pains.

The historical St. Patrick is sort of irrelevant to St. Patrick's Day. The revered man was not Irish at all, but a fourth-century Briton of a Christian Roman-British family. He was kidnapped by Irish pirates and taken as a slave to Ireland, where he became fascinated with his captors. After he escaped and returned to Britain, he vowed to return and bring the Irish into the fold of Christianity. He was ordained a priest and later consecrated as a bishop. He established churches throughout Ireland from his base in Armagh. Christianity spread throughout the island, largely due to Patrick's tireless, focused efforts to convert the pagans. Were Patrick to return from his eternal reward and arrive on Magazine Street for the St. Patrick's Day parade, not only would he see few Irish, he would be wondering whether the pagans had stayed converted.

Unlike other St. Patrick's Day celebrations elsewhere in the United States, the festivities in New Orleans are barely marginally connected to ethnic pride. The membership of the organization responsible for the Irish Channel parade, the Irish Channel St. Patrick's Day Committee, has a minority of the ethnically Irish. More than likely the "Irishman" marching along decked in beads and flowers is named Centanni, Arceneaux, or Schroeder. There are Doyles and Murphys here and there, but Irish heritage has nothing to do with St. Patrick's Day in y'at Catholicism.

The St. Patrick's Day parade is usually not held on St. Patrick's Day. Only if the saint's feast day, March 17, falls on Saturday will the parade be staged that day. The parade is held on the Saturday before St. Patrick's Day, probably so that those who wish to continue the celebrations until March 17 can do so. A parade on the Saturday before St. Patrick's Day is, according to the Irish Channel St. Patrick's Day Committee, insufficient homage to be paid to the man who converted the pagan Hibernians to Christianity. On Friday, eight days before the St. Patrick's parade in the Irish Channel, the committee has a "practice" parade, a march through the Central Business District. If Mardi Gras is very late, this practice parade will be held on the Friday after Fat Tuesday, which gives the penitent and the devout hardly enough time to recover from the Carnival season and for the ashes to have disappeared from their foreheads. The practice march meanders through the CBD on the late morning of a business day, which allows the pseudo-Hibernian marchers to disrupt traffic while advertising that the real parade will follow in eight days.

The official parade on the Saturday before St. Patrick's Day consists of hundreds of marchers, all men, most dressed in formal evening wear and tennis shoes, carrying loads of beads around their necks and holding Styrofoam staffs studded with green and white artificial flowers. Before the parade begins, the marchers, in the raiment of the day, gather for Mass in St. Mary's Assumption Church. This church is conveniently located at the start of the parade route and is the only functioning Catholic church in the Irish Channel. It was not, however, built to serve the Irish Catholics, but the Germans. Buried under the floor of St. Mary's is New Orleans' first canonized saint, Father Seelos, a German. It must be a curious sight for the spirit of the holy man to look on the green-colored festivities that go on over his grave. He undoubtedly never saw anything in his native Bavaria or even in the Irish Channel of the nineteenth century resembling a contemporary St. Patrick's Day Mass and parade.

As the marchers head up Magazine Street, various vehicles accompany them to provide the necessary liquid refreshments and portable facilities for disposing of all that necessary liquid. Following the marchers are the floats, leftovers from Mardi Gras that have been hastily, and usually inadequately, modified to reflect some theme vaguely associated with St. Patrick. For example, a float that has a papier-mâché figure of Elvis Presley will become part of the Irish Channel parade by adding a green derby hat and sash. That quickly, the float's theme becomes "Elvis Celebrates St. Patrick's Day."

Although the float riders throw Mardi Gras beads and trinkets to the crowds in the street and on the balconies, the most exciting part of the parade is the tossing of cabbages. Hundreds of cabbages fly through the air challenging the cabbage catchers to avoid sprained fingers and wrists; some are as big as volleyballs. These cabbages are usually brought to the floats in mesh sacks directly from the produce distributor, with the heavy outer leaves and dirt from the fields still on them. Both the tossers and the catchers get gritty and grimy, but what's a little dirt when so much honor is being paid to such a great saint? In addition to cabbages, some float riders toss the ingredients for an Irish stew—potatoes, carrots, onions, and bell peppers.

All these flying vegetables have religious significance. The tradition of free food falling from the sky is very ancient, going back to the Israelites being fed in the Wilderness of Sinai by manna that came from above. The New Testament relates the story of the thousands who followed Jesus and became hungry. In one of his most famous miracles, Jesus fed the multitude with seven loaves and a few fish. The St. Patrick's Day float riders also feed the hungry multitudes, but flying vegetables replace the bread and fish. As gritty and grimy as the airborne vegetables are, they're probably better as parade throws and last longer than bread and fish.

Celebrations in honor of Ireland's patron saint continue on the actual date of his feast day, March 17. There is a Mass—a very crowded, noisy Mass—in St. Patrick's Church on Camp Street. Some of the faithful will have been celebrating long before Mass, and they arrive to worship the Lord in green party attire and nicely fortified with liquid refreshments. One year the homilist was New Orleans auxiliary bishop Dominic Carmon, one of the most dignified and refined clerics in the archdiocese. He was introduced, somewhat patronizingly, as a "descendant of slaves," which was supposed to identify him with St. Patrick, who spent several years as a slave. The bishop finished his sermon with a good smile and the statement that is particularly true in New Orleans, "On St. Patrick's Day, everyone is Irish." A cheer went up from the faithful of the congregation, and the spirits-fueled fumes from their breath was lofted to heaven. Who knows, maybe God is Irish on St. Patrick's Day, too.

St. Joseph's Day

There is no point in attempting a return to Lent, yet. St. Patrick's Day is followed on March 19 by St. Joseph's Day, another important celebration in y'at Catholicism. Just as St. Patrick is associated with the Irish, pseudo Irish, and Irish wannabes, in New Orleans St. Joseph is identified with all things Italian. The Italy-St. Joseph connection is rather attenuated, however. The ancestors of the vast majority of New Orleanians who identify themselves as being of Italian heritage emigrated from the island of Sicily, not the Italian mainland. The ethnic history of Sicily is quite mixed. For example, almost the entire village of Contessa Entellina, near the city of Palermo, emigrated to New Orleans in the late nineteenth and early twentieth centuries. The descendants of these immigrants consider themselves Italian, and in New Orleans that's close enough. In historical fact, the people who came to New Orleans from Contessa Entellina were of Albanian heritage, having come to Sicily in the mid-fifteenth century, probably to escape the Ottoman Turks who had overrun that part of the world. Other Italian-Americans descend from Sicilian ancestors who were Greek, Arabic, Albanian or a combination. Nevertheless, they embrace the identity of being Italian, especially on St. Joseph's Day. Just as non-Irish y'ats enthusiastically celebrate St. Patrick's Day, St. Joseph's Day festivities are embraced by y'ats with names like Gomez, Washington, McNamara, not just those named Schiro, Centanni, and Maniscalco.

In case anyone forgot, St. Joseph is the man identified in the New Testament as the husband of Mary, the mother of Jesus. Joseph was not Jesus' biological father because Mary conceived Jesus when she was a virgin, by the power of God, before she married Joseph. Joseph had to have been a very holy man to accept the story that his betrothed had become impregnated miraculously, after a visit from an angel. Despite Mary's pregnancy, Joseph married her and went on to be Jesus' adopted father.

St. Joseph's Day is of particular importance to Sicilian-Americans, more so than to mainland Italians. The best-known of the stories connecting St. Joseph with Sicily is

In New Orleans, St. Joseph has churches, a street, an Italian festival, a huge fountain, bricks, and a bar dedicated to him.

that the saint delivered one or more villages in Sicily from pestilence and famine. In response to the prayers during the famine, fava beans grew and provided the Sicilians with sufficient nourishment to stave off starvation. The celebration of St. Joseph's Day began as a means of giving thanks to the saint for saving the Sicilians. The fava bean remains an important part of the observance.

The focal point of St. Joseph's Day is the public display of food known as a St. Joseph's altar. For days if not weeks before St. Joseph's Day, New Orleanians of Sicilian heritage and others who honor the saint and the tradition prepare ritual foods to be placed on the altars. The altar is a food offering to St. Joseph for some favor granted, often healing from sickness. Devotion to St. Joseph is in the form of a barter; if the favor sought is granted, the prayerful petitioner makes an altar to St. Joseph. This practice was until recent years very personal, with the altars erected in private homes. The altar was built in the front room or the garage. Three levels make up an altar to honor the Holy Trinity. There are many dishes placed on the altar of vegetables, fruit, and cheese, but no meat. Because St. Joseph's Day is usually in the middle of Lent, the tradition requires that the altar be meatless. There is always at least one stuffed artichoke and pastries stuffed with filling made from dried figs, sort of like a Fig Newton but much tastier. Loaves of Italian bread, called *cuchidati,* baked in the shape of crosses, rosaries, and other devotional images are placed on the altar. There is usually a cake with the image of St. Joseph on it as well. Most altars have a statue of the saint, and a large, red vigil candle.

When the altar is offered in a private home, the person who made the pledge to St. Joseph enlists the help of relatives, neighbors, and friends to prepare the foods for the altar.

The promise to St. Joseph includes a public acknowledgment, and the grateful petitioner places a classified advertisement in *The Times-Picayune* announcing that the altar is available for public viewing the night before St. Joseph's Day and on the feast day itself. When visitors arrive at the altar, they are given a piece of blessed bread and a dried fava bean, known as a lucky bean, a souvenir of the saint's having saved the starving Sicilians from death. The visitor will be told the basis of the promise: "Uncle A.J. was having real bad gout, so bad he couldn't walk. So Marie and them prayed to St. Joseph, and he walks fine now; the gout's all gone." Before any distribution of bread and beans, the altar must be blessed. Priests, preferably those with last names ending in long vowels, go from home altar to home altar, sprinkling holy water on the food and the people and usually accepting a small glass of Italian red wine.

In recent years, the tradition of honoring and thanking St. Joseph with a home altar has shifted to the erection of huge altars in public places. There is one for the public at St. Joseph's Church on Tulane Avenue, the largest church in New Orleans. The most popular altar is erected in the Piazza d'Italia, a pocket park in the Central Business District that is the site of a huge fountain dedicated to St. Joseph. Next to the piazza is the American-Italian Renaissance Museum and Library. Inside the museum is erected what has to be the world's largest St. Joseph altar. It wraps around a couple of rooms and out into a foyer. The amount of food on that one altar looks as though it alone could save a whole city in Sicily from starvation.

While the public files through the altar, with each visitor receiving a bag containing a piece of blessed bread, a holy picture of St. Joseph, and a lucky fava bean, there is a food line outside in the piazza serving spaghetti and sauce. An open-air Mass in honor of St. Joseph is offered in the middle of the day, and a band from a veterans' organization provides entertainment. The generosity, warmth, and openness of New Orleanians of Italian heritage is inspiring. At considerable expense of money, time, and energy, they open their world to the public for free. This display is a worthy and fitting homage to Jesus' adopted father.

Altars and food are not the only way to celebrate St. Joseph's Day. The setting is, after all, New Orleans. Mardi Gras has just passed, and St. Patrick's Day was just two days before. St. Joseph needs a parade, too, sometimes more than one. Although the parades honoring St. Joseph are not as large as a Mardi Gras parade or a St. Patrick's Day parade, they are lively, marching parades through the French Quarter.

Perhaps the most exotic tradition of honoring St. Joseph is the appearance of the Mardi Gras Indians. Beginning in the late nineteenth century, when traveling Wild West shows visited New Orleans, groups of black working-class men got the idea to dress as American Indians, form tribes, and march through the streets on Mardi Gras in their costumes. The costumes are elaborate and expensive to make, and showing them on just one day seemed to be a waste of efforts. The Mardi Gras Indians saw that the Italians were cavorting and partying during Lent on St. Joseph's Day, and they decided to join in the celebrations by making an appearance in the streets on St. Joseph's eve, the night before, and on St. Joseph's Day. In recent years, as the tribes became more numerous and the costumes more elaborate, the Indians decided to hold a parade of all tribes on the Sunday before St. Joseph's Day, referred to as Super Sunday. Super Sunday is usually the Sunday before St. Patrick's Day too, and the city is in a party mood. The range and flexibility of Catholicism are demonstrated in this event: a pious Galilean carpenter of 2,000 years ago is honored by groups of black American men dressed in stylized garb of North American Indians in a noisy parade through city streets. St. Joseph probably looks down in approval from his celestial reviewing stand and salutes the marchers with a hearty "Well, alright!"

Fridays in Lent

Fridays in Lent are some of the most joyous days on the y'at Catholic calendar. They are not supposed to be joyous at all. The official church designated them as days of abstinence from meat to encourage penitential practices and to remind the faithful of what Jesus gave up for sinners. In addition, Ash Wednesday and Good Friday are days of fasting on which good Catholics are to consume just one full meal. They may eat two small meals, but no snacking. The practice of fasting during Lent is based on the scriptural account of Jesus spending forty days fasting and praying in the desert before he began his public ministry. The forty days of Lent recall his period of preparation. The restriction on the consumption of meat is an ancient Lenten practice. There are, however, exemptions and exceptions from the rule. Children under age fourteen are not obliged, and neither are those who are ill or hospitalized or serving on active duty in the armed forces. Although meat, including poultry and game, cannot be consumed, fish and shellfish are permitted. In order to fully and thoroughly understand the y'at celebrations of Fridays in Lent and the restrictions and exemptions of the rule of abstinence, it is appropriate to discuss the intertwining relationships among four seemingly unrelated historical events and people: a great sixteenth-century sea battle; Miguel Cervantes's *Don Quixote;* Jean Lafitte, the pirate who was a hero of the Battle of New Orleans; and the sacred totem of the Houma Indians of South Louisiana.

In the sixteenth century, the Ottoman Turks were threatening to capture western Europe. They had already conquered eastern Europe up to Vienna, Austria, and their navy of powerful galleys dominated the eastern Mediterranean Sea. The pope, Pius V, was worried lest the Turks capture Italy and send Christianity into another decline and more turmoil as the Reformation was sweeping northern Europe. In those days, the popes were temporal rulers as well as head of the church, and Pius V allied his army and navy with those of King Philip II of Spain and a fleet of galleys from the independent city-state of Venice. This great combined fleet of nearly three hundred ships was commanded by Don John of Austria, King Philip's half-brother. On October 7, 1571, the opposing navies engaged each other in the Gulf of Patras, an arm of the Mediterranean Sea, near Lepanto, Greece. After a violent and bloody clash between the fleets, the Christians prevailed, capturing or destroying hundreds of Turkish vessels. To reward the Spanish sailors and soldiers, who apparently were the difference in achieving victory, the pope declared that all Spain would be exempt from the church's rules of fasting and abstinence. The Spanish, who were already well established in the New World, took the exemption with them across the Atlantic Ocean. By the time the Spanish took over Louisiana from France in the mid-1760s, they had long since stopped worrying about the Church's rules on fasting and abstinence.

Among the Spanish warriors who fought in the Battle of Lepanto was a young soldier named Miguel Cervantes. In the battle, he lost his left hand to a Turkish scimitar, a terrible price to pay to be excused from following the rules of fasting and abstinence. Years later Cervantes would write one of the greatest novels in history, *Don Quixote,* an insightful and shrewd commentary on life in which idealistic knight Don Quixote and his cynical squire, Sancho Panza, ride through the countryside seeking justice and truth.

At one point in the story, Sancho is made governor of the fictional island of Barataria. The word is apparently a sixteenth-century Spanish pun because the root word of Barataria means a fraud, deceit, or joke. An early French colonist in Louisiana, Claude Dubreuil, was fond of reading Don Quixote and probably had a sense of humor because, when he surveyed the swamps and marshland across the Mississippi River south of New Orleans, he named one area Barataria Island. The name was also given to the main waterway through the region, Bayou Barataria, and to the estuary between the marshes and the barrier islands, Barataria Bay.

The islands at the southern end of Barataria Bay are Grand Terre and Grand Isle, and it is there that the mysterious and notorious Jean Lafitte established his headquarters for raiding ships in the Gulf of Mexico and selling smuggled goods to the people of Louisiana. Lafitte and his henchmen received a pardon for their crimes in exchange for participating as soldiers in the Battle of New Orleans and for supplying General Andrew Jackson with needed flints for his army's firearms. Many of Lafitte's henchmen returned to Barataria after the war and resumed their outlaw ways, however. Their descendants still live in the region today, and for generations have earned a legitimate living through fishing, trapping crabs, and trawling for shrimp, which they sell to the seafood markets of New Orleans.

Although the Spanish colonists were not attuned to the

Church's rules on fasting and abstinence, the French who preceded them were, at least to some degree. But the problem of noncompliance with the rules of abstinence had a serendipitous resolution. New Orleanians could observe the Church's rule against eating meat on Fridays by partaking of the abundant seafood from the Barataria region. Fridays became the day for crabs, oysters, shrimp, and fish that were brought to the city's markets on boats that plied Barataria Bay and Bayou Barataria. By the middle of the twentieth century, the Friday night seafood dinner was a tradition for families of y'at Catholics. The commemoration of the day of Jesus' suffering and death could be done by substituting a meat meal with, for example, an oyster poor-boy (ERS-tuh PO-boy). The occasion provided an opportunity for parents to instruct their children in one of the truths of the Catholic Faith:

> "Mama, I want weenies and chili for supper."
> "You can't eat no meat today; it's Friday. You eat meat and you go to hell. We're going out to Bucktown to eat fried shrimps and seafood gumbo and soft-shell crabs."

It is important for a child to learn that a Friday in Lent is a day of sacrifice.

So attuned were y'ats to observing Fridays as days of eating seafood, that when the rule relaxed after Vatican II to abolish mandatory abstinence from meat except on Fridays in Lent, most didn't notice and went on eating seafood on Fridays, especially Fridays in Lent. Many, many restaurants built their reputations on the seafood served on Friday nights, the traditional night for families to go out to eat. The attitude of y'ats toward Fridays in Lent is succinctly stated in a sign on the wall of Charlie's Seafood, a venerable restaurant on Jefferson Highway: "Every Friday Is Good Friday Here." No one said penance couldn't taste good.

Vatican II in the 1960s coincided with the spread of the popularity of eating crawfish and the beginning of a large commercial crawfish industry. It just so happens that Lent and the height of crawfish season overlap. During Lent, it seems, the crawfish grow fat but their shells have yet to become thick and hard. They are thus much easier to pick and eat than they are later in the season. The combination of the tradition of Fridays as days of seafood with the availability of large amounts of crawfish at seafood markets and

The message at Charlie's Seafood Restaurant on Jefferson Highway is the soul of Y'at Catholicism.

the y'at practice of observing every possible event with a lot of food has made Fridays in Lent days of great rejoicing.

So where do the Houma Indians and their sacred totem come in? The Houmas, whose descendants live south and west of New Orleans in Jefferson, Lafourche, and Terrebonne parishes, are a Choctaw-speaking people who called themselves *Saktee-Homa, Chakiuma* or *Shakchi-humma,* which means "red crawfish" in their language. The name got shortened to Houma, meaning "red." The Houma people honored the crawfish as their totem, the spiritual ancestor from which they all descended. The crawfish was thus sacred to them, a sacramental creature. Modern-day y'ats, when they eat crawfish, are therefore participating in an event that was holy to the pre-Christian Houmas. Fridays in Lent thereby become doubly holy, and the crawfish taste wonderful no matter what religion you follow.

On Fridays in Lent there are long lines outside seafood markets as y'ats line up for crawfish, boiled and live. Fridays in Lent are also a time when many parochial schools hold a "Fish Fry" as fund-raising events. Catfish, oysters, and shrimp, deep fried and served with french fries and cole slaw, help the devout y'ats contemplate the passion and death of Jesus and incidentally raise a little money for the parish school.

The proliferation of a great variety of seafood in Louisiana creates an occasional discussion about just what is and what is not seafood and can be eaten on a Friday in Lent without breaking the rules. A generation or two ago, frog's legs were often seen on restaurant menus, and the question arose whether frog qualifies as seafood. That debate is nearly moot now, as frog's legs seem to have gone out of vogue. No so with turtles, however. Turtle soup is on the menu of all fine New

Orleans restaurants, and *tortue sauce piquante* (turtle with spicy sauce) is prepared in home kitchens. In recent years, the marketing of alligator meat has forced the question of whether eating alligator on a Friday in Lent violates the no-meat rule. These questions spawn discussions reminiscent of the Pharisees' interpretations of the Jewish law, which Jesus pointedly criticized. In determining what is permitted and what is prohibited by canon law, y'ats do not have any Pharisees to consult, so they tend to consult each other. The following is a hypothetical dialogue between a customer and the proprietor at hypothetical A.J.'s Seafood Market on a Friday in Lent in the Archdiocese of New Orleans.

Customer: Where y'at, A.J.; you got any trout today?

A.J.: No trout today. I got some nice drum, some shrimps, some turtle meat. I even got alligator.

Customer: Hey, today's Friday. Can't eat no meat on Friday in Lent.

A.J.: Turtle meat and alligator ain't meat. It's fish, seafood. Like crabs or oysters.

Customer: How you know that?

A.J.: Father Mangiapane says so. I pass that on to all my customers.

Father Mangiapane may not have told A.J. that interpretation directly. A.J. *may* have once heard from somebody else that the priest said so. And it may have occurred years ago, before Father Mangiapane passed away. But the story serves the purpose of interpreting the Friday-in-Lent rule. In y'at Catholicism, the study and practice of canon law is a folk art.

Palm Sunday

Several years ago, probably as a reform following Vatican II, the Catholic Church officially designated the

Sunday before Easter as Passion Sunday, dropping the traditional name of Palm Sunday. This name change was to
emphasize that the Gospel reading of that day is the recitation of the Passion of Jesus. No one calls Palm Sunday
Passion Sunday. Older Catholics remember that Passion
Sunday was the Sunday before Palm Sunday, and it was
the day on which the statues in the church were covered
with purple cloths that were not removed until Holy
Saturday. That practice went out with Vatican II, but Palm
Sunday is still what y'ats call the Sunday at the beginning
of Holy Week.

There are a lot of palm trees in New Orleans. There are
also a lot of decorative palm shrubs that grow in front
yards. The fronds from the trees are too big and too high
up to cut for Palm Sunday celebrations, so the shears get
out on the shrubbery. Many New Orleans churches have
discovered the dwarf palmetto native to south Louisiana
swamps to be an easy and economical method of providing
the congregations with palms for Mass. Each palmetto
frond is stripped so that the individual narrow parts of the
big leaf are given to each worshiper. Having a small piece
of palmetto prevents problems of members of the congregation poking themselves or their pew mates in the eye
with a full-size leaf from a yard palm shrub.

Every year there is the question, "What do we do with
the Palm Sunday palms after Palm Sunday?" Most y'at
Catholics know that the palms are blessed and are therefore considered sacramentals that should not be tossed
into the garbage can. They also know that some of the
palms, after they are dried, are burned to make ashes for
Ash Wednesday. Instead of throwing it away or turning in
the old, dried palm to the rectory for incineration, the
standard y'at practice is to stick it some place in the

house: behind the crucifix on the wall of the house, behind a picture on a dresser, or prop it in a vase made from an old hurricane glass acquired many years ago from Pat O'Brien's Bar. The old palms seem to droop and crumble after a few months, and then they somehow disappear from the house.

Palm Sunday at St. Louis Cathedral can set up a scene that is a street-theater production of a pun worthy of Shakespeare. When the palm-carrying Mass-goers leave The Cathedral, they are confronted by the many artists, performers, and clairvoyants who set up stands around Jackson Square. A palm-carrier can have a palm read before crossing the square for a cup of café au lait.

Holy Thursday

There is an old Creole tradition in the observance of Holy Thursday that is somewhat on the wane. This is the practice of eating gumbo z'herbes on the day of the Last Supper. The church observes Holy Thursday with a solemn celebration, the Eucharist of the Lord's Supper, during which twelve parishioners are chosen to sit before the altar and have the presiding bishop or priest wash their feet, a reenactment of what Jesus did for his apostles as a gesture of affection and humility before eating his last meal. The Last Supper is commemorated on Holy Thursday as the event at which Jesus instituted the Holy Eucharist, changing the bread and wine into his body and blood. It is one of the most solemn and important days on the liturgical calendar, and it begins what is called the Easter Triduum, the three days that lead up to Easter Sunday.

Why gumbo z'herbes is associated with Holy Thursday is unclear. The dish is unlike the more familiar gumbos made with seafood or with chicken and sausage. The name is Creole patois for *gumbo des herbes,* which translates literally as "gumbo of grass." It is sometimes called *gumbo vert* or, in English, "green gumbo" because it is made with a variety of greens, but no grass. One traditional story about gumbo z'herbes is that it should be made with twelve different types of green-leaf and green vegetables to honor the twelve apostles who ate with Jesus at the Last Supper. Most written recipes do not include twelve separate green vegetables, but the most important aspect of gumbo z'herbes is that it is green, very bright green.

Gumbo z'herbes usually starts with a stock made from beef or ham, although some cooks leave the meat out so that the gumbo can be eaten on Good Friday too. It is not that difficult to prepare the dish with twelve green vegetables, especially if a large amount is made. All recipes call for spinach, cabbage, and at least one other green-leaf vegetable such as collard, turnip, or mustard greens. To those five can be added the green-leaf Swiss chard and beet greens. Other green vegetables that go into gumbo z'herbes are green pepper, green onions, celery, and fresh parsley and thyme. That makes twelve if all go into the pot. After the greens are cooked down and flavored with garlic and allspice, the concoction is made into a purée and served very hot over rice and sprinkled with gumbo filé. Even without using the twelve different greens, some spiritual benefit will probably flow to the cook who makes gumbo z'herbes.

Gumbo z'herbes wasn't served at the Last Supper on the first Holy Thursday, but it's an interesting and tasty way to observe the solemnity of the day. At the Last Supper, Jesus commanded his friends to "love one another as I have loved you." Serving gumbo z'herbes to friends on Holy Thursday is a good way to show you love them.

The Creole tradition of Holy Thursday gumbo z'herbes is observed publicly at Dooky Chase Restaurant on Orleans Avenue in Tremé. The green gumbo is on the menu on that day. Lawyer William Rittenberg, who is not Catholic or even Christian, religiously goes to Dooky Chase's for lunch every year on Holy Thursday for a bowl of gumbo z'herbes. He once declined to have lunch with a colleague from out of state, an observant Jew, telling the surprised visitor that he had to have gumbo z'herbes in observance of the tradition. The out-of-towner was mortified that a Jew would be observing a Catholic holy day. Bill explained that the fact that the day was a Catholic holy day was not the point. The importance is that, "it's Holy Thursday, and you eat green gumbo on Holy Thursday." As he explained before, in New Orleans even the Jews are Catholic.

Good Friday

In y'at Catholicism, Good Friday is the biggest of the Fridays in Lent. Many businesses are closed, and good y'at Catholics observe the strict prohibition against eating meat on the solemn day by buying, boiling, and eating more crawfish than on any other day in the year. Of course, no seafood markets are closed, and customers line up and wait at the markets for hundreds of pounds of crawfish to be boiled or for trucks to arrive from southwest Louisiana loaded with bags of live crawfish. The demand for crawfish on Good Friday is so great that most seafood markets will not sell to a customer who has not placed an advance order and paid a deposit. Backyard burners are soon roaring with propane fuel under the big pots of water in which the crawfish will be cooked. Washtubs are filled with clean water to purge the live crawfish, that is, to let them gurgle and spit in clean water to get the dirt and debris out before they are thrown live into the boiling cauldrons. It is a fitting dramatic, liturgical pageant: thousands of live crawfish, the sacred totem ancestors of the Houma people, are sacrificed through ritual boiling alive on the day that Jesus Christ was put to death to redeem the people of the world.

Y'ats do more than boil crawfish on Good Friday. The tradition of walking the stations of the cross, "makin' da stations," as a y'at would say, is popular. This devotion of fourteen stations recalls the journey that Jesus made after being sentenced to death by Pontius Pilate. Each of the fourteen stations marks a step in the agonizing path from Pilate's house to Calvary Hill along the Via Dolorosa. Most of the observances of the stations of the cross are done inside churches, where the stations are visually displayed on the walls. Some are done outside. For a few years, a group of Catholics who were active in the peace-and-justice movement walked the stations of the cross through the Central Business District. They modernized the theme of the devotion to make each station a contemporary event or social condition that needed a remedy, by action as well as prayer. The practice did not draw many traditional y'at Catholics, even though it had some of the aspects of a street parade. Most y'ats preferred to "make the stations" the traditional way.

Another traditional devotion that is performed on Good Friday is the ritual of praying in nine different churches. The significance of the number nine is probably lost in the mists of medieval numerology, which includes the novenas and the nine First Fridays. For several generations, New Orleans Catholics have made a nine-church pilgrimage on Good Friday morning. The night before at the Holy Thursday celebration of the Last Supper, the consecrated hosts are removed from the main altar in the church so that the altar can be stripped bare. To prepare properly for the solemn observance of Good Friday, the church must be a stark reminder that everything was taken from Jesus after his condemnation. His clothes, his dignity, and eventually his life were forcibly seized. The bare church symbolizes his aloneness. The consecrated host is moved to a side altar or an alcove of the church that serves as a repository of the sacrament until it is distributed during communion on Good Friday afternoon or evening. There is no Mass on Good Friday, and there is no act of consecration of the bread and wine. Communion is from the bread that was consecrated on Holy Thursday. On Good Friday mornings the churches are open to permit the faithful to enter and worship before the Blessed Sacrament as it rests in the repository. This is the occasion for the nine-churches pilgrimage. The purists who follow the nine-churches tradition say that the circuit must be walked, just as Jesus walked the way of the cross. Some of the routes to reach nine churches on Good Friday morning without becoming totally exhausted are handed down from one generation to the next. There are uptown routes and downtown routes. Some of the churches that are visited are not officially parish churches but chapels. Some of the pilgrims pray while walking, others walk in silence. Those who are unable to walk the distance drive. There have been some Good Fridays on which groups of female walkers were uneasy about some of the neighborhoods through which they had to walk on their route. Rather than do the nine churches the easy way in vehicles, they hired an armed security guard to walk with them.

There is a legend associated with the tradition of the nine churches and the St. Roch Cemetery. It was said that unmarried young women who made the nine churches on Good Friday and left a donation at each church would find a husband by the end of the year. For best results, the ninth church should be the chapel of the St. Roch Cemetery. The young women would pick a four-leaf clover growing in the cemetery, a plant different from other four-leaf clovers in that there were red spots on the leaves. The story behind those four-leaf clovers is romantic, Gothic, and tragic. Once upon a time, a bride-to-be was widowed before her wedding. Despondent and devastated, she committed suicide on the grave of her betrothed. Her blood fell on the graveyard's four-leaf-clover patch, forever marking the leaves with the splatters of her exsanguination. Blood; death; Good Friday: they all go together. It's a good story.

A discussion of Good Friday cannot conclude without noting an important, tragic, historical event. On March 21, 1788, Good Friday, the city of New Orleans nearly burned to the ground. At that time, the city consisted of mainly what is now called the Vieux Carré, and the only building left undamaged was Ursuline Convent. A report from that time blames the fire on a devout lady who had lit candles at a home shrine in observance of the day. In a display of legalistic rigidity, the priests of St. Louis Church (it was not yet a cathedral) would not allow the bells of the church to be rung to sound the alarm because of the prohibition by church law of ringing bells on Good Friday.

Easter

The most important, most solemn, most joyous celebration of the Catholic liturgical calendar is observed by New Orleanians in much the same way that other American Catholics do. There is the Easter vigil service on Holy Saturday evening at which adults are baptized and received into full membership in the Catholic Church. Easter Sunday is a time for new clothes and Easter egg hunts. Restaurants have special menus and buffets to attract family groups as on Mother's Day and Thanksgiving. Gentlemen in white linen or seersucker suits are seen at Mass for the first time since the previous Easter. Easter Sunday afternoon is also a time for a big family crawfish boil if there was none on Good Friday or Holy Saturday. On Easter Sunday, unlike Good Friday, the crawfish boil pot can have sausage or wieners in it to soak up some of the seasonings along with the potatoes, corn on the cob, onions, garlic, mushrooms, and artichokes. The strong smell of "crab boil," the prepared mixture of spices and seasonings for the cooking pot, is not unlike the pungent incense that is burned at the Easter vigil service. For both crab boil and incense, the smoke and vapors rise upwards, toward God, acknowledging his majesty with pleasing aromas.

Easter has been a traditional occasion in many places for ladies to wear new hats, stylish or gaudy, large or small. What connection there is between fancy hats and the resurrection of Jesus from the dead is tenuous at best. The new hats and clothes are probably a tradition of springtime that attached itself to Easter Sunday celebrations. New Orleans is a parade town, so an Easter parade, six and a half weeks after Mardi Gras and even sooner after St. Patrick's Day and St. Joseph's Day, is in keeping with how y'ats observe religious events.

For many years the Easter parade was organized by Germaine Cazenave Wells, the proprietor of Arnaud"s Restaurant in the French Quarter. She was the daughter of "Count" Arnaud Cazenave, the founder of the establishment. Wells's parade, like the one on Fifth Avenue in New York, consisted of open mule-drawn carriages moving through the Vieux Carré until they arrived in front of St. Louis Cathedral. The ladies would alight in their finery for noon

Mass, after which the carriages would return them to Arnaud's, where they would have a glass or two or more of champagne and brandy milk punch before dinner, all done in celebration of the fact that Jesus had risen from the dead.

After Wells died, there were differences among her parading ladies as to who should be in charge of organizing the Easter parade. The Friends of Germaine Wells staged a parade, and so did another group. French Quarter entertainer and cabaret owner Chris Owens, who is not Catholic, also got into the fray and has a similar parade. Her parade does not go to the Cathedral for Mass, which is good. It would be unladylike, to say the least, if competing women in big hats arrived at the same time and jostled each other for entry into the church and for pews inside.

Hurricane Season

There is no period on the liturgical calendar designated as "hurricane season," but all y'ats are as conscious of the fact that hurricane season runs from June 1 to November 30 as they are that Lent runs from Ash Wednesday to Easter. Everyone pays more attention to daily weather reports than at other times of the year, especially in the peak hurricane months of August and September. There are the annual dire warnings from the National Weather Service about the catastrophic effects of a major hurricane striking the Louisiana coast. Those warnings became real on August 29, 2005, when Hurricane Katrina hit and levees broke, flooding 80 percent of New Orleans and all of St. Bernard Parish. Y'ats are scared when a hurricane threatens. The television weather forecasters every year advise the public of the precautions to take, the items to have on hand in the event of a storm, and the evacuation routes that will be available. Y'ats either ignore the warnings or prepare thoroughly. Those who prepare emergency supplies know to include candles for use if the electricity goes out. Y'at Catholics have traditionally included in their hurricane kits blessed candles, the ones from the February 2 blessing or from somebody's baptism. During a storm, a devout y'at will light a blessed candle even if the lights haven't gone out and say a prayer to Our Lady of Prompt Succor. She who saved New Orleans from the invading British gets the call when the city is threatened by invading tropical storms. Even if no storm is threatening, many churches in the Archdiocese of New Orleans petition Our Lady of Prompt Succor for protection during the hurricane season at the prayers of the faithful at Sunday Mass.

St. Rosalie's Day

For several months of the long, hot, New Orleans summer and the early fall there is nothing on the liturgical calendar to cause a celebration. The church observes the Umpteenth Sunday in Ordinary Time week after week. It is just as well that there are no occasions for parades and other festivities because it is just too hot. Julie Smith, a New Orleans writer of mysteries, expresses well the mood of summer: "New Orleans could wreck your liver and poison your blood. It could destroy you financially. It could shun you or embrace you, teach you tricks of the heart you thought Tennessee Williams was just kidding about. And in August it could break your spirit." The school year starts in late August, followed by Labor Day, as y'ats watch the weather reports not just for hurricane news but with hope and prayer in their hearts that summer will end in September.

As September begins, right around Labor Day, Italian-American y'ats have a procession in honor of St. Rosalie. The procession is held in Kenner, which was once a rural area settled by Sicilian immigrants who set up small farms and dairies there. The Sicilians brought their devotion to the saint with them from the old country. Rosalie or Rosalia was a twelfth-century hermit, the daughter of a nobleman who traced his ancestry to Charlemagne. She lived in a cave in the mountains above the seaport of Palermo, meditating and praying. When the plague threatened to destroy the city, the residents came to Rosalie and asked for her prayers. She complied, and the city was spared. She died in the cave, and her remains were buried in the cathedral at Palermo. The church calendar marks her feast day as September 4.

In the late 1890s an epidemic of anthrax was threatening the cattle of the Sicilian immigrant farmers near New Orleans, in both Kenner and Marrero on the West Bank. The pious folk remembered that St. Rosalie once stopped a plague in Sicily, and they again invoked her assistance with Providence to stop the anthrax. The prayers worked, the cattle were spared, and the farmers promised that St. Rosalie's intercession would be commemorated every year with a procession. The St. Rosalie's Society was founded, and every year since the anthrax was curtailed, on the Sunday following September 4, the descendants of those farmers carry a statue of the saint in a procession in Kenner, praying and giving praise to her. A church in the West Bank community of Harvey is dedicated to St. Rosalie.

Red Mass

The annual Red Mass is a liturgy sponsored by the St. Thomas More Catholic Lawyers Association and held every year in St. Louis Cathedral on the first Monday in October, which is the traditional date in judicial and legal circles for the opening of the courts' session. It follows the practice of the United States Supreme Court, which does not have a Red Mass but holds its first arguments of the session on the first Monday in October.

The name Red Mass suggests that it is an event of paradox, a Communist Mass. It's not *that* strange, but it is a Mass for the judges and lawyers of Louisiana. One needn't be a New Testament scholar to read that lawyers were the people whom Jesus often preached against. He took in a hated tax collector, Matthew, as his first apostle, and the others were lowly working men and fishermen. There wasn't a lawyer in the group. St. Luke, to whom is attributed the third gospel, was a physician, but there were no known lawyers in the early church leadership. It was not until the sixteenth century that a lawyer did something holy enough to be declared a saint by official canonization. Thomas More, the patron saint of lawyers, was the lord chancellor of England under King Henry VIII in the sixteenth century. When Henry divorced his wife, the pope refused to recognize the dissolution of the marriage. Henry then declared himself head of the church in England and asked the clergy and ministers for a pledge of loyalty. More declined and offered his resignation. That wasn't what the king wanted from his lord chancellor, and More was indicted, convicted of treason, and executed by beheading. He was canonized in 1935 by Pope Pius XI. It is a curious coincidence that two traditional earlier patron saints of lawyers were also beheaded. In the early third century, St. Catherine of Alexandria and St. Genesius of Rome, neither of whom was a lawyer, were martyred by beheading and later named patrons of lawyers.

The Mass for lawyers is called the Red Mass simply because that is the color of the vestments of the bishop, priests, and deacons who are participating in the liturgy. Red is the traditional color for a Mass invoking the inspiration of the Holy Spirit. For example, the vestments worn on the Feast of Pentecost and at the sacrament of Confirmation are red. Both formal celebrations invoke the Holy Spirit. A Mass invoking the inspiration of the Holy Spirit is also used to start the school year at Catholic schools and universities, but only the lawyers refer to it as a Red Mass.

The Red Mass in St. Louis Cathedral is another pleasant and cheerful display of the cavalier attitude of y'at Catholicism toward the Constitution's requirement of separation of church and state. Although not officially sponsored by the Bar Association or the Louisiana Supreme Court and attendance is voluntary, all judges are invited to take part and wear robes to Mass. Because all judges in Louisiana are elected except for federal judges, most show up to gather before Mass in Jackson Square, press the flesh, schmooze with their colleagues, see and be seen, and march up the center aisle of the cathedral. Some of the judges and lawyers are Catholic, but some are not Christians at all, and probably some do not even believe in God, but the Red Mass is an event to be attended. The cathedral is filled with lawyers, especially the litigators who appear in court before those judges. As the procession moves up the aisle with dozens of judges in robes, the scene has the appearance of a graduation, but without the processional music of "Pomp and Circumstance" or the Grand March from Verdi's opera, "Aida." Perhaps the judges and the church leaders feel comfortable in each other's presence. The church is a hierarchical institution, and the tradition of the hierarchy of judges (the law is what the judge says it is unless reversed by a higher court) must go well with it. And then there is the old story about the man who died and went to heaven. As he was checking in with St. Peter at the gate, he noticed a man in a white beard strolling through the celestial corridors, dressed in a long, black robe. "Who is he?" asked the newcomer. St. Pete replied, "Oh, that's God. He thinks he's a federal judge."

Fall Fairs

The early fall is the usual time for church and school fairs throughout the Archdiocese of New Orleans. They generally employ the same format, with booths selling homemade cakes and pastries, as well as plants. There are booths to test skill, such as throwing a ball at a target to dunk a brave volunteer into a tank of water that is usually a little chilly. There is music and sometimes baby contests. Some of the fairs invite crafters to set up shop, and a fairgoer can buy rosary bracelets and some of the most tacky and kitsch religious gimcracks imaginable. You may have to look around a bit, but there is probably even something depicting Jesus as a biker among all that amazing stuff.

Many church fairs contract with companies to provide portable carnival rides. These companies travel from fair to fair with their Ferris wheels, tilt-a-whirls, fishing ponds and a lot of other attractions, all manned by employees who all look as though they were born with unfiltered cigarettes in their lips and have never lived anywhere other than in an old recreational vehicle, except for those times when they were in jail. It is to such people that parochial-school parents entrust their children's safety as they climb aboard the carnival rides. All these activities are to raise money for church and school projects.

Many of the fairs have recurring themes, such as the Pecan Festival at St. Rita in Harahan. Because there are so many fall festivals in the New Orleans area, a listing of all of them is difficult if not inaccurate as some change from year to year. One of the biggest and most successful has been staged annually for more than thirty years. Holy Guardian Angels Parish in Bridge City, at the West Bank end of the Huey P. Long Bridge, is the home of the Gumbo Festival. This event has become so large, so popular, and so successful that tiny Bridge City, an unincorporated area dominated by the Avondale Shipyard, the bridge, and railroad yards, is touted as the "Gumbo Capital of the World." For many years, the profits of the festival went into constructing a parish center. At first there was just a concrete slab, then came steel columns supporting the roof. Every year something was added until a large community center was constructed. The festival even has its own permanent site, Gumbo Festival Park at Angel Square, even though the festival is just one weekend a year. There are the usual carnival rides and booths, but the main attraction is gumbo, lots and lots of gumbo, more than two thousand gallons of gumbo. There are two kinds of gumbo sold at the festival—seafood and chicken and sausage. The two thousand gallons of gumbo probably require a half-ton of rice, too. On Friday night there is a race across the Huey P. Long Bridge as part of the festival. More than eight hundred runners and walkers struggle up and down the bridge and then replenish their energy at the end with, what else, gumbo. Live music all weekend helps the gumbo go down smoothly.

All Saints Day

November 1 is one of the big days in y'at Catholicism.

The Feast of All Saints in most American dioceses draws little interest, with few attending Mass, falling as it usually does on a weekday. A movement began among some American bishops to move the feast day to the first Sunday in November so that more Catholics would attend, a proposal that was vigorously quashed by the archbishop of New Orleans and other Louisiana bishops. There is no need to move the feast day to Sunday in New Orleans because for many Catholics and businesses it is a holiday as well as a holy day. Continuing a tradition that was brought from France, New Orleans Catholics prepare for All Saints Day by ensuring that their family tombs and the graves of their departed loved ones are cleaned and weeded, with the grass cut. In past generations, there was a practice of applying whitewash, a mixture of lime and water, to the above-ground tombs on the days before the Feast of All Saints. Modern masonry paint, which lasts longer than whitewash, has done away with that tradition, but inspecting and renovating tombs and graves remains an important preparation for the holy day.

On Halloween or on the morning of All Saints Day, flowers are placed on the graves and tombs. There are silent prayers for the dead, as y'at Catholics believe sincerely in not only life after death but also the closing clause of the Nicene Creed, the resurrection of the body. There is the vague expectation that on the day of final judgment all those fancy and expensive tombs will open up and the dead souls will rise in a special way in a nonphysical body to unity with God. The purpose of a holy day honoring all the saints is to give recognition and veneration to those who have died and have not been made official, canonized saints of the Catholic Church. Everyone knows someone who is or was a saint in the estimation of others. Some are family members, some are people who have inspired those around them.

The practice of visiting the graves of the dead on All Saints Day has been vigorously encouraged by a spiritual-commercial combination of the Archdiocese of New Orleans and the cemetery industry. The commercial cemeteries use the day for promotion, and the Church uses the attendance in the graveyards as an occasion for the special liturgy of the holy day. Many cemeteries, especially those owned by for-profit corporations, sponsor an open-air Mass on the grounds on November 1. Observant Catholics can visit the tombs of the dead and attend holy day Mass in the same location and as they leave the cemetery get a promotional brochure urging them to pay now and die later.

The feast day was set on the Catholic calendar on November 1 to coincide with the ancient pagan Celtic festival of Samhain. Samhain was the last day of the Celtic year, a day on which the dead could cross over into life again. The Celts used the day to honor their dead ancestors. This pagan tradition and the Christian devotion of honoring the dead as saints went together well. The holy day was once called the Feast of All Hallows, an old term for the saints. The night before was observed as All Hallows Eve, which eventually became Hallowe'en or Halloween. In visiting the burial sites of deceased family members on All Saints Day, y'ats are participating in an ancient tradition that is not limited to the pagan Celts' observance of Samhain. The veneration of ancestors is a common practice in many ancient cultures as well as modern ones. It has been said that New Orleanians are much like the traditional Chinese; they both eat a lot of rice and worship their ancestors.

The importance of All Saints Day to New Orleans culture is also shown in the name of the city's National Football League team, the Saints. The team's corporate existence dates from All Saints Day 1966. The theme song of the team is the traditional jazz spiritual "When The Saints Go Marchin' In." The combination of the team's being named for a Catholic holy day and the jazz hymn is strong manifestation that Catholicism and New Orleans are culturally indivisible. Other teams in the National Football League are named for wild animals (Bears, Lions, Jaguars), criminals (Buccaneers, Raiders), and gold seekers (Forty-Niners), but only the New Orleans Saints are named for holy heroes who have made it to heaven. Despite never having made it to the Super Bowl in nearly forty years of trying, the significance of the name Saints is not diminished. What other team has fans who show up for home games dressed as the pope or Moses?

The month of November closes the liturgical year, and the first Sunday of Advent begins the next one. The rhythm of the year is a comfortable feeling for y'at Catholics, a deeper, cerebral version of the satisfying cadence of a New Orleans brass band leading a street parade.

CHAPTER 8

Education

Parochial school is an integral part of the Catholic experience in America. In the past, girls in pleated, navy-blue skirts or jumpers and boys in khaki shirts and pants were immediately identifiable with Catholic school. Sometimes the colors of the uniforms are different, but the experience is the same. For several generations that experience was learning academics as well as discipline from a surprisingly large conglomeration of nuns, brothers, and priests. Hardly anyone could know all the different orders of sisters and identify them by their habits. There seemed to be dozens if not hundreds of separate groups of these educators. Sisters with simple veils, sisters with flaring wimples. Brothers and priests in cassocks, priests with Roman collars, brothers with straight black ties;, friars in brown robes, priests wearing birettas. Nuns, brothers, and priests were never seen in public except dressed in their clerical attire. It was no different in New Orleans.

Catholic-school education began within a few years of the city's founding in 1718. Capuchin Father Raphael de Luxembourg set up the first school on St. Ann Street, but it lasted only a few years. In 1727, the Ursuline nuns arrived from France and began a school for girls, a school that is still teaching girls today in grades prekindergarten through high school. Catholic education in New Orleans has grown ever since. The Sisters of Mount Carmel, Brothers of the Holy Cross, Christian Brothers, Sisters of St. Joseph, Marianites of Holy Cross, Dominicans, Jesuits, Redemptorists, and many other orders of religious women and men have left indelible marks on not only the education of New Orleanians, but on their personal identities as well.

So good were some elementary parochial schools that their excellence created problems for the admissions directors. The archdiocese long had a policy that children were to attend the parochial school associated with the church parish in which they resided. Popular, excellent schools such as Holy Name of Jesus, next to Loyola University, and St. Catherine of Siena at Bonnabel Boulevard and Metairie Road had to screen some of their applicants to make sure they were geographically eligible. Real-estate salespeople would list homes for sale with the added information of church parish. After stating the address and size of the house, the listing might add "Holy Name Parish!" The reputation of the schools improved the property values of the neighborhood. After many years of lots of exceptions and spotty enforcement of the policy, a student's residency in the geographic area of the church parish is no longer required for attending that school.

It is, however, in New Orleans Catholic high schools that y'ats find permanent cultural and social identity. More so than in other places in America, New Orleans natives identify themselves and each other by where they went to high school, especially if that high school is Catholic. In a New Orleans Catholic high school, a y'at comes of age, binding with others who are also going through a four- or five-year initiation into an important sub-group. You learn the phrases, voice patterns, and body language that will serve as subtle marks of your identity for a lifetime.

Flying on an airplane at thirty-five thousand feet or sitting in a restaurant in Chicago, one y'at may hear a voice nearby whose distinct phrases, rhythm, intonations, and syntax mark the speaker as a New Orleanian. The y'at may approach the speaker, ask if he or she is from New Orleans, and when the question has been answered affirmatively and a few introductory pleasantries exchanged, someone will always ask, "Where'd you go to high school?" The answer to that question provides a wealth of information about the person just met. For instance, the answer "St. Aloysius," or simply "Aloysius," tells you that the speaker is a man who graduated from high school no later than the mid-1960s, when St. Aloysius, an all-boys high school run by the Brothers of the Sacred Heart, was closed. The answer also reveals that the St. Aloysius alumnus probably lived in the downtown neighborhood below the French Quarter or in Gentilly. An Aloysius answer also reveals that his parents were probably working-class people who were joining the middle class in the post-World War II period. The answers "Cor Jesu" or "Brother Martin" are equally revealing. Cor Jesu, which means Heart of Jesus in Latin, was established by the Brothers of the Sacred Heart in the 1950s to serve the boys who were residents of the then-expanding Gentilly neighborhood. When the brothers closed St. Aloysius in the 1960s, Cor Jesu and St. Aloysius merged to form Brother Martin High School, named for Brother Martin Hernandez, at the site of Cor Jesu on Elysian Fields Avenue. The "Elysian Fields" is an ironic address for an institution dedicated to preparing teenage boys for a life as good Catholic men. In classical mythology, the Elysian Fields or Elysium was the place where dead people went for a blissful afterlife.

If the person answers the question, "Where'd you go to high school?" with "Dominican," she attended the all-girls school started by the Dominican nuns. If she is middle aged or beyond, you could discreetly judge her age by asking whether she graduated from the school when it was on the corner of St. Charles Avenue and Broadway, before it moved to Walmsley Avenue next to the archdiocesan Chancery Office.

The official, full name of Dominican is St. Mary's Dominican High School, but no one calls it that. This is a good thing, because there is another Catholic high school for girls on Chef Menteur Highway in eastern New Orleans called St. Mary's Academy. (Is it incongruous that a school established to teach young girls Catholic values and principles is located on a street whose name in French means "Chief Liar"?) Dominican High School has a street named for it, the rear boundary of the old campus at Broadway and St. Charles Avenue. There is a street named St. Mary, but it is Uptown and nowhere near St. Mary's Academy.

Another way to gauge the age of a y'at woman of a certain age is if she answers that she went to high school at "Holy Name." This girls' high school was associated with Most Holy Name of Jesus Parish, which also has an elementary school of the same name. In the 1960s, however, the high school changed its name to Mercy Academy. A woman who reveals that she graduated from Holy Name of Jesus High School thus gives away her age. The same is true if she says that she went to Mercy Academy, because the school closed in the 1990s.

Identification by high school can be tricky for girls because there were two schools dedicated to St. Joseph, St.

Joseph's Academy in Gentilly and St. Joseph's High School affiliated with the parish church of the same name. There were also Academy of the Sacred Heart on St. Charles Avenue and Sacred Heart High School on Canal Street. To differentiate the two, the latter school was sometimes called Sacred Heart on Canal Street. The confusion in names was settled when all these girls' schools except Academy of the Sacred Heart, which was always considered a place for girls from families of wealth and influence, closed. Women will differentiate themselves when the inevitable "Where'd you go to high school?" question is asked and the answer is "Sacred Heart" by such comments as, "The one on Canal; my daddy was a plumber, you know."

Men who answer the question with "Holy Cross" reveal that they most likely grew up in the downtown neighborhoods or in adjacent St. Bernard Parish, although Holy Cross High School has been around for many generations and loyal alumni from all over the New Orleans area send their sons to the school, which was established by the Brothers of Holy Cross on the site of an old plantation. The venerable and respected school has given its name to the immediate neighborhood as well, the Holy Cross Historic District, whose designation as such protects it from destruction and unchecked urbanization.

Going to a Holy Cross football game for the first time can be a startling musical experience. As the team takes the field, the Holy Cross band strikes up the familiar strains of, of all things, the Notre Dame fight song. The Holy Cross High School mascot is a tiger, a long way from Ireland. However, the Brothers of Holy Cross who founded and operate Holy Cross High School also founded the University of Notre Dame in South Bend, Indiana. One fight song fits all, especially if it's a good one.

Perhaps the best-known Catholic high school in New Orleans is St. Augustine, founded in 1951 when segregation by race was the law. The Josephite Fathers established the school to educate young black Catholic men. Except when formality is desired, the school is called St. Aug by everyone. The official name also presents a question of proper pronunciation. Catholic school teachers always instruct their pupils that the name of the great saint of the early church, St. Augustine of Hippo, is pronounced *ah-GUS-tin*, not *AUH-gus-teen*. There seems to be a specific pronunciation of the saint's name that is different from the name of the city in Florida and the name of the grass on so many lawns in New Orleans. Regardless, New Orleanians generally stick to St. Aug when referring to the school. There is a St. Augustine Catholic Church and even a St. Augustine Episcopal Church, but the latter is probably named for St. Augustine of Canterbury, the sixth-century saint who evangelized the Angles and Saxons who had invaded Britain.

St. Aug High School became a great success, educating and creating a Catholic middle class of black men and Creoles of color. Those young men became leaders in their professions and in politics. But the greatest success of St. Aug is its marching band, the "Marching 100." In true New Orleans tradition, the "Marching 100" has more than one hundred members, but nobody cares. The music is spirited and brassy. The marchers are disciplined, and their uniforms are neat and distinctive. The band is in demand to lead Mardi Gras parades, as well as parades in other cities. All y'ats look forward to seeing the St. Aug Marching 100 at the front of a parade because their presence is a signal that the parade is going to be a good one.

One wonders what St Augustine would think were he to

return to earth and find himself on St. Charles Avenue as the St. Aug Marching 100 struts past, horns calling and the crowd cheering and dancing. Augustine was from Hippo, a coastal Mediterranean city in what is now Tunisia. Although his mother, St. Monica, was a Christian, his father was a Roman and a pagan. Augustine was a bit of a libertine and liked partying and good times. He did not embrace Christianity until he was well into adulthood. He then became one of the most influential figures in Christianity. Partly as a result of the debaucheries of his earlier years, his writings show a strong suspicion—if not a complete rejection—of what Catholic moral writings tend to call pleasures of the flesh. What changes might he have made in his theology had he watched, heard, and felt the sensuous beat of the St. Aug Marching 100 leading Rex down St. Charles Avenue on Mardi Gras?

Jesuit High School has been a bastion of Mid-City at South Carrollton Avenue and Banks Street since 1926, when it moved from downtown on Baronne Street, where it had been since its founding in 1847 as the College of the Immaculate Conception. The loyalty of Blue Jay alumni for their all-boys school and each other is legendary. Third- and fourth-generation sons, grandsons, and great-grandsons are part of the network that extends well beyond the city. The alumni count among their members many priests, politicians, and professionals. If a would-be stranger answered "Jesuit" to the where'd-you-go-to-high-school question and if the questioner was also a Jesuit graduate, that one-word answer provides a powerful communication link and a sense of shared tradition and pride.

The Christian Brothers have run a high school for boys on St. Charles Avenue since the early 1950s. In the 1990s, as many of the girls' Catholic high schools were closing, the school began admitting girls. The Brothers named the school for the founder of their order, St. Jean-Baptiste de la Salle, as De La Salle High School. Some y'ats pronounce the name of the school *DEE-la-sal,* but loyal De La Salle students and alumni give it the French pronunciation of *DEH-LA-SAL.*

There is one now-closed Catholic high school that identified itself with its neighborhood more than any other. Redemptorist High School and the Irish Channel went together like beans and rice. At a time when Catholic high schools in New Orleans were either for boys or girls, Redemptorist was the only coeducational Catholic high school in the archdiocese.

As the New Orleans suburbs expanded in the 1950s and '60s, the archdiocese began to build Catholic high schools to serve those residential areas. The older schools in the city had been built by religious orders and were named for saints or the name of the orders, such as Holy Cross, Ursuline, Jesuit, and Dominican. The archdiocese decided that it needed to honor former archbishops, so the new schools were named for men who had served the archdiocese but weren't canonized saints. Whether any of them ever become canonized saints is unlikely—not that they were unworthy but because there is no movement to canonize any of them—so the schools will never have a "St." designation. The schools are Archbishop Shaw for boys and Archbishop Blenk for girls on the West Bank and Archbishop Chapelle for girls and Archbishop Rummel for boys in Metairie. Of course, hardly anybody refers to the schools using the "Archbishop" prefix. The short answer of "Shaw" or "Chapelle" to the question, "Where did you go to high school?" identifies the person as a suburban y'at born after 1948.

The identity of a y'at by high school is so strong that it stays with the person forever, providing a means of recognizing each other even after years away from New Orleans. The following is a true story of how that takes place.

A middle-age woman and her husband, both professional people in the Cincinnati suburb of Fort Thomas, Kentucky, were watching television one evening. She is a native New Orleanian who attended Dominican High School. He is neither Catholic nor a native New Orleanian. They had been living away from New Orleans for thirty years. The television talk show featured Richard Simmons, the fitness and exercise guru, as a guest. Simmons began to talk about growing up in New Orleans and attending Catholic high school. Simmons did not at first say the name of his alma mater.

The expatriate New Orleans woman began an analysis of the scene—Simmons's age, his speech pattern, the inflexions, his body language. "He did not go to Holy Cross or Jesuit or De La Salle," she said. She turned to her husband and confidently stated, "Richard Simmons went to Cor Jesu." "How'd you know that?" asked her astounded mate. The woman smiled confidently. A few minutes later Simmons told the show's host that the high school he attended was no more, having been merged with another under the name Brother Martin. His high school, Simmons said, was Cor Jesu. The husband got up and fixed himself a drink.

For many y'ats, choosing a high school is not a matter of discussion:

"Your paw-paw went to Holy Cross, your parrain went to Holy Cross, and I went to Holy Cross. You're going to Holy Cross."

"You gotta go to Dominican. Your Aunt JoAnn joined the Dominican sisters, changed her name to Sister Matilda, then changed it back to Sister JoAnn. If she did all that, you'll hurt her feelings if you don't go there."

For families without the generational connection to a high school, the choice is more difficult:

"I know all your friends are going to Rummel, but Brother Martin's a better school for you. Besides it's closer. Rummel's way out there in Met'ry."

Uptown on Magazine Street is the girls' high school known as Xavier Prep. The full name of the school, which no one uses except in formal writing, is Xavier University Preparatory School. The school has very catchy initials that are displayed on the girls' band uniforms as they march and play in carnival parades—XUP. How is that pronounced? Is it pronounced? Maybe *eks-up* or *zup?*

A discussion of Xavier Prep requires a discussion of the university that Xavier Prep is a preparatory school for, Xavier University of Louisiana, named for St. Francis Xavier, a contemporary follower of St. Ignatius Loyola, founder of the Society of Jesus. Francis Xavier was a remarkable missionary, bringing Christianity to India and Japan. The traditional y'at pronunciation of the saint's name, *egg-ZAVE-ya,* is generally not heard on campus. The correct pronunciation is *ZAVE-yer.* Like Sts. Augustine, Bernard, and Jean-Baptiste de la Salle, the correct pronunciation of the saint's name is a distinguishing characteristic of Catholic education. Xavier University is the only Catholic university in the United States that was founded for the purpose of educating black students, who at the time of the school's founding in 1925 were prohibited by law from attending school with white people. It is also the only university in the United States founded by a saint, St. Katherine Drexel, who is discussed later in the book.

Xavier University has dedicated itself to education in

the biological and health sciences. Its premedical program produces a greater number of black students accepted into medical schools than any other college. Its pharmacy school is the only one in Louisiana south of the University of Louisiana at Monroe and turns out dozens of well-prepared druggists every year. They fill prescriptions even for people who pronounce Xavier *egg-ZAVE-ya.*

In Algiers, "over the river," as y'ats say, is Our Lady of Holy Cross College, founded by the Congregation of Marianites of Holy Cross. This order of nuns is the female side of the Order of Holy Cross, founded in France in the mid-nineteenth century. The brothers run Holy Cross High School. The Marianites have long been a strong influence in New Orleans education, staffing several elementary schools and the Academy of the Holy Angels, a high school for girls in the Bywater neighborhood below the French Quarter that closed in the 1990s. Our Lady of Holy Cross College fills an important spot in New Orleans education. It is the only four-year college, private or public, on the West Bank.

The largest y'at Catholic institution of learning in New Orleans is Loyola University (pronounced *lye-O-la*). Officially its name is Loyola University New Orleans, which was changed from it long-time official name of Loyola University of the South. The name distinguishes it from Loyola University Chicago and Loyola Marymount University in Los Angeles. The Jesuits like to name their institutions of higher learning after their founder, St. Ignatius Loyola. At the time of its founding in the early twentieth century, Loyola was the only Catholic college in the Deep South. However, the South covers much territory, and Loyola University of the South could be, if one didn't know better, in Birmingham or Biloxi or the Okefenokee

Swamp of Georgia. To pinpoint the school geographically, the Jesuits changed the name to Loyola University New Orleans. This change was very fitting because Loyola is not culturally Southern; its most recent name identifies it as a true y'at center of learning. The Web site of the university proclaims that it is both "Catholic and Jesuit." Perhaps the Jesuit fathers, who take a lot of verbal jabs, felt that identifying Loyola merely as "Jesuit" would not be sufficient information, inasmuch as there are some people who think that the Jesuits are not, or should not be, part of the Catholic Church.

Loyola is the y'at Catholic power center. Generations of New Orleans Catholics have become dentists, bankers, lawyers, pharmacists, stockbrokers, scientists, doctors, and judges because of their Loyola educations. Nevertheless, Loyola often has had an image problem because it abuts the campus of Tulane University, a private, secular institution that is larger than Loyola and has a wider national reputation. In the center of the Loyola quadrangle facing St. Charles Avenue is a white, life-size statue of Jesus, robes flowing and arms and hands lifted in prayer. Various interpretations of the meaning of the statue have been made for as long as there have been students at both Loyola and Tulane. The general gist of one Tulane interpretation is that Jesus' posture indicates that he is saying something like, "It's not my fault that Tulane is next door!" Loyola students, on the other hand, nicknamed the statue "Touchdown Jesus." However, after years of aloofness if not downright suspicion between the two universities, the ecumenical spirit and openness following Vatican II has permitted more cooperation between the two.

CHAPTER 9
Saints and Not-Quites

From the earliest days, New Orleans Catholicism has produced some notable characters, some of whom have become canonized saints. Heroism and holiness have mixed with intrigue and defiance. Men and women who have influenced New Orleans Catholicism came in the earliest years, and holy and influential Catholics continue to invigorate the city. The Ursuline sisters came to New Orleans from France just a few years after the city was carved out of the swamps and natural levees between the Mississippi River and Bayou St. John. The Ursulines' presence has continued ever since, more than two hundred and fifty years of teaching the young women of New Orleans.

It is difficult to imagine what went through the minds of those twelve idealistic nuns as they disembarked in the summer of 1727 wearing their heavy, woolen habits that were appropriate for the cool climate of northern France. Their voyage from France was long and dangerous, including a brush with pirates. The ship did not make it all the way to the city. The nuns had to be transported up the Mississippi River in pirogues. They undoubtedly were escorted by swarms of mosquitoes.

The streets of New Orleans were muddy, often filled

with water. The sidewalks, where there were some, were wooden. There was no drainage system or sewerage system. The smell in midsummer probably would have made them gag had they not been so busy slapping mosquitoes. In the fall of 1727 they opened a school for girls without regard to race or social standing. Indian and African girls were taught as along with the daughters of the white colonists. They also sponsored an organization of lay women called the Children of Mary, a confraternity of women who pledged to take special care to educate their slaves in Catholicism and treat them properly. These educational efforts were the origins of the practice of Catholicism among New Orleans' black citizens. The Ursulines' bravery and heroic efforts to bring Catholic education and piety to what was then a teeming swamp must surely qualify them for notation in the ledgers of heaven.

The first Ursulines were led by a mother superior with the interesting name of Marie Tranchepain. Her family name means bread slicer. The early Ursuline sisters might have been considered "the greatest thing since sliced bread" by the struggling colonists in 1727 because there were no schools or systematic care for the sick and the poor until they arrived.

In 1781 a group of Capuchin friars arrived in New Orleans from Spain. Among them was one Fra Francisco Antonio Ildefonso Moreno y Arza, who was a native of Sedella in the Granada region of Spain. He became known as Padre de Sedella because of his hometown. In 1785 he became pastor of St. Louis Church, not yet a cathedral. Unknown to the civil authorities, including Governor Esteban Rodriguez Miro y Sabater, in 1787 Padre de Sedella was made the Louisiana commissary of the Spanish Inquisition, the agency of the Catholic Church dedicated to locating heretics and unbelievers, including American Protestants, and converting them to the true faith. In 1788, King Charles III of Spain, at the urging of the colonial governors, prohibited the Inquisition in the colonies because of its negative effect on recruiting settlers for the colonies who were not Catholic. Governor Miro particularly wanted the Inquisition banned because he was actively seeking American immigrants for Louisiana as buffers against British expansion. Miro was a practical man, and he knew that most Americans were not Catholic and that they should not have to face the feared Inquisition when they entered Louisiana.

Padre de Sedella was apparently a true believer, however, and chose to ignore the king's proclamation. He asked Governor Miro for soldiers to help him carry out his duties as the commissary of the Inquisition, and the governor became furious. Miro had the priest arrested. Padre de Sedella tried to supersede the governor's arrest order by invoking his authority as the commissary, but the plan didn't work. The troops who were supposed to enforce the Inquisition obeyed the governor and stuck the angry friar on a ship back to Cadiz, Spain. Two years later Governor Miro returned to Spain for a promotion. Some say that Padre de Sedella was instrumental in the reassignment that got Miro out of Louisiana.

Padre de Sedella did not go gently. Back in Spain he plotted his return to New Orleans. He apparently had influential connections in Madrid and elsewhere, because in 1795 he was cleared of all charges and back at his former post at St. Louis Church. Padre de Sedella's timing and procedures were exquisite. Governor Miro was gone, and Louisiana had been named a separate diocese, no longer reporting to the bishop in Havana as it had done previously. Padre de

Sedella assumed the familiar name of Padre Antonio, Père Antoine to the majority French-speaking New Orleanians. Wealthy philanthropist Don Andres Almonester y Roxas had provided the funds to build a cathedral, and there was a new bishop in residence, Luis Peñalver y Cardenas. The new bishop stayed until 1801, when he was elevated to the position of archbishop of Guatemala. He was not replaced, leaving a void in the church hierarchy in New Orleans into which Père Antoine eagerly entered.

In 1803 Louisiana was transferred to France, and Napoleon promptly sold it to the United States. The diocese of Louisiana, with no bishop, was ripe for ecclesiastical skullduggery. An Irish priest who had been educated in Spain, Father Patrick Walsh, was the vicar of the diocese and nominally in charge following the departure of Bishop Penalver. Walsh was no friend of the popular Père Antoine. Father Walsh and Père Antoine got into a vicious power play, with Walsh sending communication to the bishop in Havana that Père Antoine was a troublemaker and was foisting schism among the faithful. Père Antoine was creative during the period of confusion. Always popular with the laity, he had himself elected pastor of St. Louis Cathedral by the congregation.

In 1805, the pope placed Louisiana under Bishop John Carroll of Baltimore, the only United States bishop at the time. Bishop Carroll did not trust the Spanish schemer, and he sent Father Louis William Valentin Dubourg, a Frenchman born in Saint-Domingue and a refugee, first in Spain and then in Baltimore from the French Revolution, to New Orleans to be the administrator of the diocese of Louisiana. Father Dubourg was a political animal in his own right. Father Walsh, the diocesan vicar, conveniently died in 1806. Father Dubourg jockeyed into position, and when General Andrew Jackson needed help in gathering forces to repulse the British invasion in 1814, he assisted greatly. He also greeted General Jackson at the door of the cathedral when the general returned victorious from the Battle of New Orleans. It was Father Dubourg, not Père Antoine, who celebrated the victory Mass. Dubourg had upstaged the popular Spanish friar, and he was later appointed bishop of Louisiana in 1815.

Although Père Antoine had sworn allegiance to the United States before Governor W. C. C. Claiborne, he secretly continued to exercise his allegiance to the king of Spain. The revolutionary spirit was rapidly spreading over Spanish America, and there were many plots. Spain was losing its grip on its colonies as Simon Bolivar led rebellious armies in South America. The notorious Lafitte brothers, Jean and Pierre, who had preyed on Spanish ships as pirates and privateers, became secret agents of Spain in exchange for pardons for their piracy against Spanish interests. Just like James Bond, the Lafittes had code numbers. Pierre was Numero 13, and Jean was Numero 13-B. They learned later that the Spanish intelligence service was still active in Louisiana, by 1812 a state of the United States, and that its chief was Antonio de Sedella, better known as Père Antoine. The Lafitte brothers, at the cleric's direction, were instrumental in thwarting the plans of revolutionary General Francisco Xavier Mina to invade Mexico.

Père Antoine remained enormously popular in New Orleans. Most people did not know or did not want to believe that he was an agent of the Spanish crown. His reputation among the people of New Orleans was that of a holy and generous pastor who cared deeply for his flock. Even years after his death, some chroniclers have disputed that he was such a sinister character, calling the stories of his cloak-and-dagger operations lies created by his enemies. Although he did not ring the bells of St. Louis Church as an alarm for the public on that horrible Good Friday 1788, when the city nearly burned to the ground, he did organize a bucket brigade that saved the Ursuline Convent from the flames. Perhaps the finagling friar actually wanted the old church to be destroyed. It was decrepit and needed replacement badly.

His popularity and pastoral leadership must have been due to attributes other than his religious and spiritual qualities. In 1826, when Père Antoine had been the pastor of St. Louis Church and Cathedral for more than twenty-five years, Bishop Joseph Rosati, who had been consecrated coadjutor bishop of New Orleans in 1824 and was then made bishop of the new diocese of St. Louis while remaining administrator of the Diocese of New Orleans, wrote a scathing critique of the spirituality of New Orleans Catholics. He wrote that New Orleans was "a large city, the population of which is for the most part made up of unbelievers and other enemies of religion. There is a need there for a man capable of speaking the language eloquently, so as to impose respect for the Word of God and not expose it to the danger of being scoffed at in the newspapers." The inference of Père Antoine's failure as a spiritual leader is inescapable.

The controversial but greatly loved priest outlived nearly everybody. He did not die until 1829 at the age of 81. The walkway between St. Louis Cathedral and the Presbytere was named for him, Père Antoine Alley. It is a parallel match for the walkway on the other side of the cathedral, Pirate Alley, named in part for the Lafitte Brothers who were the friar's spies.

As complex and sinister as Père Antoine was, even before his death there appeared in New Orleans a woman who was the embodiment of simplicity and unfailing piety, Henriette Delille. The social structure of New Orleans in the antebellum period was stratified by class, race, and color. The white people were divided into the Creoles, French and Spanish in heritage, and the Americans—the Anglos, Irish, and Germans. The bottom of the social order was occupied by the enslaved black people. Above the slaves were the free blacks, and above them but below the whites were the *gens libres de couleur,* the free people of color, also known as Creoles of color. Among people of color there was an array of social status based on lightness or darkness of the skin. There were mulattoes, griffes, quadroons, and octoroons. There were those who were *passant blanc,* passing for white. In this matrix of color, people were to be aware of their place and behave in accordance with that status.

The free people of color were generally French-speaking, Catholic, and had much in common with the white Creoles. They downplayed their African ancestry. Some of the Creoles of color were successful merchants, tradespeople, craftsmen, and artisans. Some were wealthy and well respected by all levels of the complex New Orleans social order. Henriette Delille was a Creole of color. She was given a fine education and trained to be a gentlewoman. She could "pass" and could have become the pampered mistress of a wealthy white gentleman.

Despite the wealth, good manners, and education of the Creoles of color, they could never move into white social circles, as race was too volatile a question to permit such freedom. Segregated seating at public events was the rule, but it was not taken well by everyone. When the first passenger trains came to New Orleans in 1831, the seats were segregated by race and color. This resulted in a race riot in 1833. In this mixture of superficial gentility and tension, Delille saw the need for service to those denied basic education and social services. She rejected her expected place in society and began to work with the free and the enslaved blacks, visiting the sick and elderly, assisting the poor, and instructing young girls in basic education. In an embarrassment to her family, she openly rejoiced in that part of her heritage that was African. In 1836, she and two other women, also Creoles of color, began to organize their burgeoning ministries. By 1841, their efforts were recognized and encouraged by the institutional Church, and in 1842 they established the group as an official order of nuns, the Sisters of the Holy Family. Delille used her wealth to buy a house for the sisters to live in, from which they conducted their educational and social ministries to the poor, elderly, and dying. Delille's piety was uncomplicated and straightforward. Her guiding principle was, "I believe in God. I hope in God. I love God. I want to live and die for God." She died in 1862.

The Sisters of the Holy Family are still active in New Orleans and throughout the United Sates and Central America. In New Orleans, the sisters operate St. Mary's Academy, a girls' high school they founded in 1880 for young ladies of color. Delille has been formally proposed for canonization, a long and bureaucratic process. She has been given the title Servant of Slaves, and the tedious work of documenting all that she did and verifying miracles attributed to her is underway. This work is unnecessary for devout y'at Catholics; they don't need people in the Vatican to tell them that Henriette Delille is a saint. It will nevertheless be satisfying to the Sisters of the Holy Family and to all who honor their foundress to add the official title of Saint to her name one day. St. Henriette Delille, the first canonized saint born in New Orleans.

When Francis Xavier Seelos was baptized the day he was born in Fussen, Bavaria, his parents wanted to give him a head start toward sainthood by giving him the full name of one of the best-known saints. Francis decided to be a priest early in life, but he did not enter the Jesuits, the religious order of his namesake. He first entered the diocesan seminary but later was impressed by the zeal of the members of the Congregation of the Most Holy Redeemer, the Redemptorists. After joining the Redemptorists, he went to the United States to minister to German-speaking Catholics. He finished his studies in New York and was ordained in Baltimore in 1844. For the next several years he was assigned to many cities throughout the United States, starting with Pittsburgh. He gained a reputation for his simple piety and expertise as a confessor and spiritual director, as well as a novice master charged with training and forming young men for the Redemptorist order.

After traveling and preaching in German and English, Father Seelos was assigned to New Orleans in 1866 and became the pastor of St. Mary's Assumption Church, the German church in the Irish Channel. He immediately became known as a deeply caring pastor, ministering to the poorest and sickest people in that poor section of the city. He was there in the midst of a yellow-fever epidemic, caring for the sick and dying, when he, too, came down with the disease and died only a year after he arrived in New Orleans.

Everyone who had had contact with Father Seelos knew that he was a saint. People began directing prayers to him asking for intercession with God for sickness and other troubles. Some of these prayers were soon answered, and the news spread quickly. New Orleans Catholics of subsequent generations learned that the holy man was a good person to pray to, and the long, arduous process of having him officially declared a saint began. The power of Father Seelos, as he was and still is known to New Orleanians, to perform miracles from beyond the grave was attested to, and the case for his sainthood was presented to the Vatican. In April 2000, Pope John Paul II declared Father Seelos to be Blessed Francis Xavier Seelos, one step away from officially and canonically becoming a saint. During the process, the remains of Father Seelos had to be exhumed twice. He had been buried under the floor of his parish church in the Irish Channel, but one of the requirements of the Vatican before a holy person can be canonized is to dig up the remains and check to see if they are really there and that the coffin had not been disturbed. A photographer documented every step of the exhumation process. There is no DNA check, however; the Vatican has not gone that far yet.

In October 2000, the remains of Father Seelos were exhumed for the second time and carried to the cathedral for a repeat of his funeral, this time with the archbishop as principal celebrant. He was taken back, with a police escort that he did not have at his first funeral, to St. Mary's Church where, it is hoped, he will rest in peace without being dug up again. The old Latin Mass for the dead, which was used at Father Seelos's first funeral in 1867, begins *Requiem aeternam dona ei Domino,* "Lord, give him eternal rest." One hopes the saint will now be allowed to rest in his grave in peace.

There is a center and museum in honor of Father Seelos at St. Mary's Assumption Church. There, you can get a booklet of prayers for a novena to the holy man dubbed the Cheerful Ascetic.

Just as Henriette Delille was raised in comfort in ante-bellum New Orleans, Katharine Drexel was raised in financial comfort in Philadelphia. She was born in 1858, but her mother died only a month later. Her father was very wealthy, but he was a very devout man and gave generously to many charitable organizations. He married again, and Katharine's stepmother was also a generous and devout Catholic. Despite the wealth and her life of ease, Drexel wanted to become a nun and enter a cloistered, contemplative convent. After her stepmother and father died, Drexel inherited, as one would say in today's term, mega bucks. She was a beneficiary of a huge trust created by her father's will. Like Henriette Delille, she was appalled at the treatment given to the nonwhite citizens of the country. At the urging of her spiritual advisor, she reluctantly gave up her plan to join a convent of cloistered nuns and instead formed a new group of nuns who would use her wealth to assist poor people, Indians, and blacks. She founded the Sisters of the Blessed Sacrament, an order of sisters who are partially contemplative, with their principal daily activities being Mass and the adoration of the Blessed Sacrament. Drexel spent her money throughout the United States establishing schools for Indians and blacks who had no other access to education.

In 1917, Drexel's generosity was showered on New Orleans, a city segregated by racial laws. She started a secondary school for black students. Two years later, she expanded that school into a teachers' college. From that base, in 1925 St. Katharine Drexel again expanded the institution into Xavier University, a liberal-arts college.

Drexel remained active in administering the many schools that the Sisters of the Blessed Sacrament had begun, even after her health declined. She died in 1955.

On October 1, 2000, Pope John Paul II canonized her, and she is now officially St. Katharine Drexel. The canonization was a formality; generations of Xavier students and alumni as well as many New Orleanians of all races knew for a long time that she was a saint. The city of New Orleans honored her on the day of her canonization by renaming the street in front of Xavier University Drexel Drive. St. Katharine is the first person associated with New Orleans to be canonized fully and declared an official saint of the Catholic Church.

At about the time of St. Katharine Drexel's death, a great conflict was beginning to erupt in New Orleans that would involve three powerful Catholic men. The first of these was Archbishop Joseph Rummel, who had been consecrated Archbishop of New Orleans in 1935. In 1953, he issued a directive to all parishes entitled "Blessed Are the Peacemakers." In that pastoral letter he ordered that all forms of segregation that were practiced in Catholic churches and other institutions be stopped because such discrimination was morally wrong.

Archbishop Rummel's proclamation was radical for racially segregated New Orleans. Resistance to desegregation was already building in response to President Truman's policy of integrating the armed forces and other agencies of the federal government. The archbishop stopped, however, at implementing a plan to desegregate immediately. Segregation by race was required by law, and those laws had not yet been declared unconstitutional. The reaction of many white people to the pastoral letter was vigorous and negative. Belief in racial segregation was deeply ingrained in the white people of New Orleans, Catholics included, and they thought the archbishop was straying too far away from his job description.

The next year, 1954, the United States Supreme Court issued its famous decision in *Brown v. Board of Education of Topeka,* in which the court declared that racial segregation in public schools, the so-called "separate but equal" doctrine, was unconstitutional because the school systems were inherently unequal. Archbishop Rummel could now proceed with the desegregation of New Orleans Catholic schools, churches, and other facilities. Even before the laws were declared unconstitutional, the archbishop had become the first Catholic bishop in the southern United States to accept black candidates for the priesthood into the archdiocese's seminary.

The doctrine of "separate but equal," struck down by the court in *Brown,* had originated in an earlier decision that had arisen in New Orleans. In 1892 Homer Plessy, a New Orleans Creole of color—the reports describe him as being one-eighth black and seven-eighths white—bought a train ticket in New Orleans to go to Covington, Louisiana, on the north side of Lake Pontchartrain. He boarded the train and sat in the section reserved for whites only. He was told that he had to sit in the section reserved for blacks, and he refused, whereupon he was arrested, convicted, and fined. He took the case to the U.S. Supreme Court, which at that time ruled that laws providing for "separate but equal" facilities did not violate the U.S. Constitution.

In 1956, Archbishop Rummel, now legally buoyed by the *Brown* decision, in another pastoral letter announced that racial segregation in Catholic schools was morally wrong. He did not, however, order quick and immediate desegregation. This lack of resolve disappointed many people in the archdiocese who thought that the schools should open their doors to children of all races right away.

Catholic segregationists in New Orleans were outraged by the *Brown* decision and the archbishop's decree to desegregate the schools. They found a powerful and eloquent leader in Leander Perez, known as Judge Perez. Judge Perez was a brilliant constitutional lawyer and the political boss of St. Bernard and Plaquemines parishes. He was also extremely wealthy and owned a home on one of the most exclusive streets in New Orleans. He made his views heard in such segregationist organizations as the White Citizens Council and openly and vigorously denounced the mingling of the races. Other Catholic voices came forward, publicly adding their support for maintaining the racist practices that had been in place since the founding of the city of New Orleans.

In Judge Perez's fiefdom of Plaquemines Parish, there is a small community with the unusual name of Jesuit Bend. It is a semirural area in a bend of the Mississippi River. There were no Jesuits in Jesuit Bend in 1955, although the community's name comes from the fact that the Jesuits first settled the area in the early 1700s. Archbishop Rummel assigned a black priest to a mission church parish there, but the white members of the congregation revolted and refused to allow the priest to assume his duties. Archbishop Rummel then invoked a procedure rarely used in modern times. He placed the church under diocesan interdict, a process that closed the church and denied the racist congregation a place to worship and access to the sacraments. The interdict of a group is roughly comparable to the declaration of anathema or excommunication against an individual and is an extremely serious and drastic punishment. The archbishop showed that he would not be bullied by Judge Perez and the segregationists, who had much sympathetic support at the time.

Due to Archbishop Rummel's advanced age and failing health, Pope John XXIII appointed Archbishop John Cody as coadjutor archbishop in 1962. He was soon to be the third man in the Catholic power struggles over desegregation of the Archdiocese of New Orleans. Shortly after taking his post, Archbishop Cody ordered that all Catholic schools in the archdiocese be desegregated at once. The gradual and slow process, with delays and stalls, that had been the desegregation process in New Orleans was to end. Loud protests again came from Catholic segregationists. In one Catholic church, the priest's sermon at Sunday Mass was on Jesus' commandment that all Christians love one another. The priest pointedly stated that this commandment applied to racial harmony and that whites and blacks should accept one another in an integrated society, as Jesus directed. Some outraged members of the congregation stood up in protest, while one parishioner demanded that the priest stop his sermon or he would leave. The priests said nothing in response and continued the sermon, further annoying the bigot. The man then left with a few sympathizers, calling back into the church "If I miss Mass today, it's your fault!" Such was the attitude of some of the Catholic "faithful" during those difficult times.

Perez and some other vocal opponents of racially integrated Catholic schools went so far as to write to the Vatican for assistance in restricting the archbishop's decree. That went too far. It was one thing to oppose integration, but it was something more serious under canon law to oppose the archbishop's authority to teach Catholic doctrine in the parochial schools. The Vatican soundly rejected the overtures from the racists.

Archbishops Rummel and Cody, the new man in town, decided to put the hammer down. Archbishop Rummel publicly excommunicated Judge Perez and two other vocal Catholic segregationists. That meant that they were declared outside the membership of the Church. They could not receive the sacraments until they reconciled and asked for forgiveness. Excommunication, like interdiction, is a powerful sanction that is rarely used. Those excommunications had an immediate effect on the rest of the segregationists. They shut up. They knew the archbishop meant business and that he would toss them out of the very Church they were trying to keep all-white. Years later, prior to his death, Judge Perez did reconcile and was buried in a Catholic funeral.

Archbishop Cody, who became sole archbishop after Archbishop Rummel died, had further struggles with parishes in New Orleans over control of finances, and he left in 1965 to become Archbishop of Chicago and later a cardinal. The struggle of Leander Perez and the segregationists with the archbishops was one of the ugliest periods in the history of New Orleans Catholicism. Because of the courage and forcefulness of Archbishops Rummel and Cody, New Orleans Catholicism survived the crisis and thrived in a new spirit of reconciliation.

For hundreds of years of church history, the determination of who was a saint worthy of veneration by Christians was a local, decentralized process. After the death of someone with a reputation for holiness, people who knew and admired him or her would begin praying for favors, building a shrine, or telling others about the life and holiness of the venerated person. The cause of sainthood really got moving if miracles began to be credited to the dead person. The venerated holy man or woman might even have appeared after death, to be seen by the believers. People would visit the home of the saint-to-be, collecting articles of clothing and other relics that might have miraculous, healing potency. Grave robbers often dug up the corpse and conducted commercial transactions in pieces of the deceased's clothing, hair, and skeleton. A local group might take up the cause and help erect a small church to house the relics. Without the requirement of approval by the pope and his administrators in the Vatican, a person could just be declared a saint by his or her community. This canonization by popular proclamation led to many holy people being declared saints. There was, unfortunately, too often abuse of the process because some dead people who were not particularly saintly or heroic got churches or shrines named for them. Some shrines were started for commercial purposes, to attract pilgrims with money to spend. This commercialism of sacred things was one of the practices that led to the Reformation.

The frauds, potential for frauds, and commercialization of relics were dealt with in the Counter-Reformation Council of Trent in the sixteenth century. Henceforth, nobody could become a saint unless the Vatican said so. The elaborate and tedious procedures and delays of those post-Reformation changes have frustrated those who knew a holy person during her or his lifetime and are utterly convinced that the hero they knew in life is now in full unity with God. However, to get a candidate for sainthood on the track for canonization requires knowledge of the Vatican processes and the funds to pay the cost of investigation, documentation, and exhumation. There were two holy, heroic people in New Orleans in the latter part of the twentieth century who, were the pre-Reformation process of sainthood still in practice, would be canonized by acclamation of the citizens of New Orleans.

Sister Lillian McCormack had a special vocation from

God to minister to special children, those with physical, developmental, and neurological handicaps. She called them her "blue roses." "If there were such a thing as a blue rose," she said, "with what care it would be nurtured! Our children need that nurturing." McCormack was born in New Orleans and entered the order of the School Sisters of Notre Dame in the early 1930s. In 1952 she started a school for special-needs children in St. Louis. It was the first such Catholic school in the country. She was transferred to Dallas in 1963 and started another school there. But Archbishop Cody had heard of the good things she was doing and asked her to come home to the Crescent City. She returned home and began the hard work of starting, from the ground up, a school for special children. She screened prospective students, their parents, teachers, and staff members. She sought out a physical location and raised money. St. Michael's Special School was ready to open in September 1965 when Hurricane Betsy devastated the city. St. Michael's was spared any serious damage, and Sister Lillian opened it a few days later, even as the city was cleaning up from the worst storm in decades.

Sister Lillian's disarming personality and straightforward devotion infected everyone who came in contact with her. She saw special-needs children not as burdens who must be endured by their families and the community, but as gifts from God who provide those who must care for them with opportunities to become closer to God. Sister Lillian's "blue roses" became a focus for the movers and shakers of the city and elsewhere to show that they had been enthralled by her cheerful, simple holiness.

Sister Lillian was, among other things, a native New Orleanian and thus knew the paramount place good food has in the public consciousness. In 1978 she inspired famous New Orleans chef Warren Leruth to organize the first "Chefs' Charity for Children." Celebrity chefs demonstrate their culinary skills for a group of people who pay a hefty price for tickets to the event. Guests get to sample the chefs' creations and to purchase souvenir cookbooks of the event. All proceeds go to St. Michael's Special School for Sister Lillian's "blue roses." The event is an annual celebration.

Sister Lillian's admirers also organize an annual "Blue Rose Ball," a fancy-dress fund raiser. Fat cats in black ties and ladies in formal evening finery pay generously for tickets knowing that St Michael's Special School is the beneficiary. More important, the ballgoers are inspired by Sister Lillian to find joy and satisfaction in the care of special-needs children.

At the urging of her supporters and with the help of Chef John Folse, Sister Lillian wrote a book about caring for special children, *God Writes His Miracles for the Other Side of the Shadow.* In addition to her own thoughts and meditations, she includes in the book the writings of parents of children who have attended St. Michael's. The effect of her warmth, optimism, and holiness on these parents is obvious. When Sister Lillian died in July 2000, everyone who had known her were ready to proclaim her a saint. They know she is; they don't need the Vatican to tell them so.

Harry Tompson was a y'at. Harry Tompson was a prophet. Harry Tompson is a saint. Every day of high school, Harry Tompson put on his khaki Jesuit uniform at his home in Algiers and crossed the Mississippi River on the ferry. As he stared at the river water, the same color as his uniform, he dreamed about wearing another uniform, the cassock and collar of a Jesuit priest. Shortly after graduating high school, Tompson fulfilled that dream and entered the Society of Jesus. During the long years of study, prayer, meditation, and the spiritual exercises of St. Ignatius Loyola, Tompson changed from a shy, unassuming teenager into a committed and dynamic spiritual and educational leader. As principal and then president of Jesuit High School, he became legendary for his caring for each individual student even though enrollment exceeded one thousand boys. He was the pastor to thousands of students, alumni, and their families. He was loud and vigorous. He was intense and insistent. He challenged everyone who came in contact with him to active holiness.

Tompson never lost his thick 1950s y'at accent. God was *GAWD*. Mary was the *bles-SED MUH-tha*. He was proud to be a y'at and reveled in the excitement of Mardi Gras. In the true y'at spirit, he rode in the Bacchus parade on the Sunday night before Mardi Gras, yelling to the crowds, showering them generously with beads as he had generously showered them with prayers. Here was a scene that would have made the leaders of the early church roll over in their graves: the best-known, most popular priest in the city of New Orleans is enthusiastically part of the celebration of the Roman god of wine and partying, one of the pagan deities against whom the church fathers had spent their careers preaching and writing.

The Old Testament prophets were frequently preachers of gloom and doom. Harry Tompson was also a prophet, but he was a prophet of joy, celebration, and generosity. His two-minute sermons are legendary in a city steeped in folklore and tradition. He challenged Christians to act as they believed, to experience the exhilaration, as he did, of service to others. In his often loud and raucous style of preaching, Tompson could inspire a lukewarm Catholic to participate in a full, vigorous life of service and holiness that was exciting and rewarding.

When he was retreat master at the Jesuit retreat house at Manresa in Convent, Louisiana, Tompson's ability to instill a sense of active, participatory holiness in men who had been passive about their religion came forth just as he had done with high-school students at Jesuit. His passion for everything he set out to do was more than just inspiring; it was a magnet that attracted others to come forth to serve God and their fellow men and women who were less fortunate. Tompson could ask, almost demand, donations from wealthy people that would make them gulp with surprise, then sit down and write a pledge or a check in the four, five, six, or seven figures that Harry was asking for. With those donations he built an addition to Jesuit High School, refurbished Manresa Retreat House, which was more than one hundred and fifty years old, and renovated the Church of the Immaculate Conception (Jesuits' Church).

His final years as pastor of Jesuits' Church were spent fighting a losing battle against cancer. Perhaps the pain and the prospect of hastened mortality focused him even more because his last building project was the establishment of the Good Shepherd Nativity Mission School. This elementary school enrolls children from the lowest stratum of New Orleans society, the children of inner-city poverty and despair. Tompson loved New Orleans and his fellow citizens so much that he wanted to reach out to the most neglected and bring those children up so that they, too, could love the city and praise God as much as he did. Tompson died a few months before the school opened, but his inspiration impelled his followers to fulfill his dream. The school stands as a monument.

Jesuit Father Norman O'Neal, a longtime colleague of Tompson's, wrote that his well-known accomplishments at Jesuit High School, Manresa, Jesuits' Church, and the

Good Shepherd School are not how he would remember Tompson. Rather, Father O'Neal remembers his dedication to ministering to those who were sick and dying. When he was notified that someone was sick or hospitalized and was calling for him, Tompson, no matter how busy or tired, would drop everything and visit that suffering friend. For Father O'Neal, this was Tompson's most intense holiness.

Harry Tompson's love and holiness were as vigorous and powerful as the Mississippi River over which he traveled and dreamed every day in high school. The heat and intensity of his commitment to helping other people were a great fire that created its own draft, drawing in everyone around him, warming them to acts of generosity and piety. Is there anyone in the city of New Orleans who would deny that Tompson is a saint, a person blessed by God? The ancient procedure for canonization should be invoked, and Tompson should be declared a saint by acclamation. He should be added immediately to the recitation of the Litany of the Saints: "St. Harry Tompson, pray for us!"

CHAPTER 10

Miscellaneous Stuff

Social Apostolate

Social services provided by New Orleans Catholics in fulfillment of Jesus' directive to do for others as they would do for him is truly impressive. The Office of Catholic Charities of the archdiocese has an annual budget of approximately twenty million dollars and serves more than fifty-seven thousand clients through nearly sixty programs. Other programs of service are administered through individual church parishes and Catholic schools. Some of the largest and most successful programs undertaken by the archdiocese include the resettlement of refugees from Southeast Asia and Central America. Wars and natural disasters have brought thousands of immigrants into the dynamic flow of New Orleans Catholicism. The many programs that provide food and housing for poor people operate constantly, not just at the time of the annual Thanksgiving baskets drives. A complete listing of all the social-service functions performed by New Orleans Catholics would be impossible. For one example of the community's commitment to caring for others, take a look at the work done at Ozanam Inn, a homeless shelter on Camp Street.

The neighborhood near the intersection of Camp and

Julia streets was once worse than a slum. It was skid row, with inhabitants suffering from severe alcoholism, mental disease, social disorder, and the poverty and despair that accompany them. Passed-out drunks slept on sidewalks, flophouses provided filthy accommodations for those with a little money, and dingy barrooms supplied booze and street wine to those whose cravings controlled their lives. In 1955, Archbishop Rummel and the Society of St. Vincent de Paul opened Ozanam Inn a half-block from Camp and Julia to provide a place of refuge for men living on the streets of the neighborhood.

The Society of St. Vincent de Paul is an organization of Catholic lay people and is named for the patron saint of charity and service to the poor. St. Vincent was born in France in 1580. He was captured by Turkish pirates while he was on a voyage in the Mediterranean and taken to Tunis, North Africa, where he was sold as a galley slave. He managed to escape and returned to France where he worked enthusiastically for years to aid the poor and downtrodden. He directed much of his ministry toward the convicts who were sentenced to the galleys, as he had been in Africa. Into a horrendous world of violence, stench, filth, and anger he brought the love of God.

In the nineteenth century brilliant French lawyer and scholar, Antoine-Frédéric Ozanam, was challenged by anti-Catholic scholars to show that Christianity had any relevance in the modern world. In response, Ozanam and a few friends began an organization dedicated to assisting the poor. They dedicated their organization to the patron saint of Catholic charity and named it the Society of St. Vincent de Paul. They set up places in France to provide care and assistance to the needy and the desperate. Since then, the society has spread all over the world and is one of the largest organizations of lay men and women within the Catholic Church.

Ozanam Inn in New Orleans is no longer on skid row, even though it has not moved geographically. Beginning in the late 1970s, the neighborhood around the shelter began to change, as the flophouses and bars were converted to offices and apartments. There was pressure from the residents of the gentrified buildings to close Ozanam Inn or move it someplace else. The Society of St. Vincent de Paul agreed to move if someone would buy the property. No buyers came forth, and the shelter continues to serve the area's homeless men, who have no place else to go. Every day nearly eight hundred free meals are served, and almost one hundred men are given free clean beds and clean clothes in a neighborhood where a fancy condominium can sell for $500,000, monthly fees not included.

Ozanam Inn is unsentimental, straight-from-the-shoulder Christian charity. The Society of St. Vincent de Paul has no romantic or unrealistic notions about whom they are serving and how they can help. The derelicts and the drug addicts, the deranged and the demented are all children of God. They are not so much homeless people as they are people whose home is the street. Most of them cannot hold down regular jobs. They have no social skills. Some of the guests at Ozanam Inn are ugly and mean. They can be angry and ungrateful. Yet, their attitudes are not grounds for rejection. Quite the contrary, they are a challenge to the practice of charity. In the lobby of Ozanam Inn near the front door is posted an admonition written by St. Vincent de Paul to his followers:

> You will find that charity is a heavy burden to carry, heavier than the bowl of soup and the basket of bread. But you must keep your gentleness and your smile. It is not enough to give bread and soup.

This the rich can do. You are servants of the poor.
They are your masters, terribly sensitive and
exacting as you will see. But the uglier and dirtier
they are, the more unjust and bitter, the more you
must give them your love. It is only because of your
love, only your love, that the poor will forgive you
for the bread you gave them.

Strong words. The followers of St. Vincent de Paul at
Ozanam Inn meet that challenge every day.

Single Y'at Catholics

In the 1950s, before Vatican II, a group of young adults
at St. Anthony of Padua Parish on Canal Street realized
that there was no ministry aimed at young, single adults
who did not go to college. In those days if a Catholic graduated from high school without going to college, going to
the novitiate for nuns and brothers, going to the seminary
for priests, or getting married soon, there was little to look
for in life. Girls without immediate prospects for marriage
might become secretaries, beauticians, or waitresses.
Young men might wait to be drafted or sign up in the
armed forces right after graduation. Some followed their
fathers or other relatives into the labor force.

The formation of the group called the Padua 20s
addressed this void. They saw some of their contempo-
raries at college, usually nearby at Loyola or the new
Louisiana State University at New Orleans, and understood
that those former high-school classmates were starting new
lives in which they could not participate. Mid-City, in
which St. Anthony of Padua Parish is located, is a mostly
working-class neighborhood. Attending college was not
economically or culturally available to the majority of the

people there. Many stayed in the neighborhood, living with parents, waiting for life to offer something to replace the thrills of high school. What they could look forward to, thanks to the Padua 20s, was a dance every month or so where they could meet friends from high school and maybe someone of the opposite sex who was fun and compatible. The shared Catholicism was a good meeting ground.

The Padua 20s dances were prime '50s popular culture. The young y'at men would slick back their hair with Brylcreem and slip on their loafers over white socks. Some blue suede shoes may have shown up at a dance or two, but white buck shoes and khaki pants were definitely out because that was the uniform of the "frats," the generic term for male collegians. Pony-tail hairdos for the young women were very popular, as were full skirts supported by several petticoats underneath and appliquéd poodles on the outside. Flat shoes were cheap, easy on the feet, and good for dancing. For several years, the Padua 20s provided a respectable place for single y'at Catholics to meet members of the opposite sex. The doo-wop and rhythm and blues music played on 45 rpm records provided a mood of sexual restraint, an atmosphere best described by 1960s comedian "Brother Dave" Gardner as, "music that makes folks wanna touch one another."

Then came the social storms and cultural turbulence of the 1960s and '70s. Vatican II changed the church, and nuns and priests began to leave in droves, The Vietnam War divided the country politically, and the civil rights movement changed the tranquil façade of New Orleans culture. The modern feminist movement began with vigor and fire as bra-burning demonstrations spread. The sexual revolution coincided with the Age of Aquarius. The comforts and strictures of 1950s Catholicism were no more. The Padua 20s became an anachronism.

But y'at Catholicism was expanding in the 1960s and

'70s, as new parishes were formed with new churches and
schools in the suburbs. In the area called New Metairie
(pronounced *NOO MET-tree*), to distinguish it from Old
Metairie, the elegant, older neighborhood along Metairie
Road, many large parishes were established. One of the
biggest and most vibrant, with many ministries and activities,
is St. Clement of Rome, dedicated to St. Peter's successor
as the fourth pope. St. Clement's ministries include an
organization for single adult Catholics. The organizers did
not come up with a catchy name like the Padua 20s—like
maybe the "Clement Times." The group is called the St.
Clement of Rome Single and Single Again Ministry. Like
the Padua 20s, the St. Clement group has monthly dances.
The group also meets for Sunday Mass and lunch afterwards. Outings and picnics are scheduled, and there is a
drama club and a scripture study group. The St. Clement
singles group has attracted attention beyond Metairie and
New Orleans, and single adults drive from the north shore
of Lake Pontchartrain and as far as Baton Rouge to attend.

One of the most positive, significant statements made by
the Single and Single Again group through its Web site is that
it is ecumenical and welcomes those who are divorced and
separated. The Catholic Church in which the Padua 20s was
formed was, at best, suspicious of single adults who were not
engaged to be married, planning to get married, or in religious life. Divorced Catholics were the equivalent of
medieval lepers. Non-Catholics and divorced people were not
welcome at the pre-Vatican II singles ministries. Those were
the days when a Catholic seeking to marry a non-Catholic
needed special permission from the bishop. St. Clement of
Rome's singles group has left those old beliefs in the past.
Another refreshing change from 1950s y'at Catholicism is
that the singles group seems to rely more on individual judgment and the inspiration of the Holy Spirit to help single

Catholics stay chaste until they enter into a sacramental marriage. In those pre-Vatican II days, the disapproval by the Church of virtually all things sexual was a real presence and pressure in the minds of young y'at Catholics.

Burying St. Joseph

Burying a statue of St. Joseph in your yard to speed up the sale of your house is a practice not unique to y'at Catholicism. Nevertheless, it has a spirit and image that merge well into the other colorful observances of New Orleanians. The belief is that if a statue of St. Joseph, the patron saint of the family and household, is buried on the premises of the house to be sold, a buyer with a good price will soon appear. The Catholic Church treads carefully around this folk practice that smells too much like super-stition. The Catholic Information Center in Washington, D. C., explains that the Church encourages devotion to and veneration of the saints, St. Joseph being one of the most universally popular, but to the extent that the practice is superstition, it disapproves. A prayer to St. Joseph is a good thing, but expecting him to be a miraculous real-estate agent is outside the official doctrine of the Catholic Church.

The practice is supposed to have originated with the six-teenth-century Spanish mystic, St. Teresa of Avila. St. Teresa and the nuns of her convent prayed to St. Joseph because more land was needed for new convents for the many new nuns and friars who were inspired by her. Her original convent at Avila was dedicated to St. Joseph, and she encouraged the nuns to bury medals of St. Joseph in the earth as some sort of offering to him. Apparently St. Joseph came to her aid, and many convents and friaries were established despite a lot of local opposition.

The modern practice of burying St. Joseph has been

embraced by real-estate brokers and agents. Some carry a supply of St. Joseph statues in their vehicles, just in case clients ask about the efficacy of the practice. To be done correctly, the statue of St. Joseph should be buried upside down in the front yard, facing away from the house. If burying in the front yard is not practical because, for instance, there is no front yard, the statue can be buried in the back yard. However, a backyard interment should be with the statue right side up and facing toward the house. Why these different methods of burying poor St. Joe came about may once again be one of the mystical, unanswerable questions that makes Catholicism fun.

The Race Horse and the Sisters

Louis J. Roussel III is a wealthy horse trainer. He is also a devout y'at Catholic. After a monumental but winning battle with throat cancer, Roussel acquired a new colt with a great deal of promise. The colt was a son of one of the greatest thoroughbred horses of all time, Secretariat. Soon thereafter, Roussel was inspired by a Christmas Mass to name the young animal Risen Star. Roussel, grateful for his recovery, promised the Little Sisters of the Poor, who ran the Mary Joseph Residence for the elderly in Algiers, that they would get 10 percent of Risen Star's winnings. Did the good sisters pray for the horse named for the star of Bethlehem to win? To place? To show? Whether they did or not, somebody's prayers were answered. In the 1988 Kentucky Derby, the first race of the annual Triple Crown, Risen Star came in third. But in the next few weeks, he won first place in the other two races of the Triple Crown, the Belmont Stakes and the Preakness. As a result, Roussel, the other owners of Risen Star, and the Little

Sisters of the Poor made a nice piece of money. The Mary Joseph Residence benefited from playing the horses. God works in strange and wonderful ways, especially in New Orleans and even at the two-dollar window.

Death: Eschatology or the Hereafter

Death does not stop the celebration. New Orleans jazz funerals are so well known that they have become another tourist attraction. Nevertheless, it is a funeral and a manifestation of the duty owed by Christians to respect the dead. The tradition of the jazz funeral calls for a slow march from the funeral parlor to the cemetery while a band plays dirges and other slow, spiritual pieces. "Just a Closer Walk With Thee" is always appropriate at this stage of the funeral. After the deceased is placed in the tomb, the music becomes loud and spirited, a point in the burial service known as "cutting him loose," that is, letting the deceased ascend to heaven. The funeral procession then becomes a street parade with lively music. "When the Saints Go Marchin' In" is the best known of the numbers played by funeral bands on the way back from the cemetery. The band and the mourners, some now dancing and carrying umbrellas, are the "first line" of the procession, and the people along the street, also dancing and carrying umbrellas, are the "second line." This division of mourners and revelers is the origin of the term now used generally to describe New Orleans street dancing.

The celebration of death in New Orleans funerals anticipated liturgical and theological reforms that came out of Vatican II. Prior to that council, Catholic funerals were dark and dismal. The funeral Mass was called the *Missa pro Defunctis,* Mass for the Dead, and the priests wore black vestments. The funeral music was minor-key ominous, highlighted by the haunting but magnificent Gregorian chant of the *Dies Irae,* the Day of Wrath. The emphasis was on the horrors associated with the last judgment. Wearing of black by immediate family mourners was nearly mandatory. But Vatican II did away with all the gloom and doom of funeral liturgy. The Mass for the Dead was replaced by the Mass of Christian Burial. Because Catholics believe that death is not the final event in life but the beginning of new life with God, the funeral, though mourning the loss of a loved one, now emphasizes the positive fact of that new life. The vestments were changed to white to represent the anticipated resurrection of the dead to union with Christ. The *Dies Irae* was stricken, despite its stark beauty, so that anyone wanting to hear it now must buy a recording. The change in funeral liturgy, a return to the original Christian theology of resurrection and celebration, goes well with the long-standing y'at tradition of a funeral as a celebration.

The tradition of the wake, once an important part of the ritual of burying the dead, has almost disappeared. The "waking of the dead," the all-night watch before a funeral, has given way to visitation just before the Mass of burial. For many y'at Catholics, the practice of reciting the rosary during the wake or visitation continues. Friends and mourners who want to offer condolence to the bereaved and pay respect to the deceased need to do so before or after the rosary, which usually takes about fifteen or twenty minutes. A respectful y'at who doesn't have much time for mourning can call the funeral home to inquire when the rosary will be recited for the deceased. Once supplied with that information, the mourner can make a brief appearance, staying long enough to shake hands, embrace the bereaved, sign the guest book, and pick up a holy card with the deceased's name and a prayer on it. Mourners with a closer attachment to the deceased or the family may stay for the full service, go to the cemetery, and maybe a lunch afterwards. All y'ats like to eat, and how better to honor the dead than with a nice muffuletta and a Barq's root beer after the service.

Catholic schools used to teach that the Catholic Church was composed of three separate groups of people: the Church Militant, the Church Suffering, and the Church Triumphant. The Church Militant are the people living on earth, "fighting" for salvation. Why salvation has to be a fight was never explained thoroughly, except to say that it is a struggle to get to heaven. The Church Suffering are the "poor souls," the people in purgatory who have died but are not yet in heaven because they still have some of the stain of sin to be cleansed from their souls before they can join the saints in heaven with the full awareness of God. The Church Triumphant are the saints in heaven, those who made it all the way through the "gates of pearl" described in the Book of Revelation.

The theological doctrine of purgatory is itself in limbo. Say the word "purgatory," and many people think of a ski resort in Colorado. Few Catholics, including y'ats, rarely think about it. November 2, the Feast of All Souls, gets little attention anymore. Y'ats celebrate Halloween on October 31, All Saints Day on November 1, and have had enough by November 2. Nevertheless, masses on All Souls Day pray for those who are doing time in purgatory to get into heaven. Like most prisoners, they get credit for good behavior.

So what happens after death? Many y'ats don't worry too much about life after death because they know, in the ancient Jewish tradition, that if you live well with the Lord during your lifetime and follow the church's teachings, the hereafter is not a cause for concern. The strange and prophetic Book of Revelation, the final book of the New Testament, says that there will be one hundred and forty-four thousand of the elect in heaven, no more, no fewer. St. John, who it is said wrote the book, had never met any y'ats. Y'ats are steeped in the eschatology of street music and know that they will make "a closer walk" with Jesus and that they will "be in that number" when the saints celebrate on the day of the final judgment of God. They will be among the saints who "go marchin' in."

A y'at might envision life after death as a parade through the pearly gates of heaven, while the strains of George Lewis's clarinet—surely a celestial sound—wail the exhilarating joy of "Just a Closer Walk With Thee." As the smell of red beans and smoked sausage wafts through the mists, the y'at greets St. Peter, "Where y'at, St. Pete!" The celestial gatekeeper smiles, pops the cap off a bottle of cold Dixie beer, and answers, "Well, all right!"

A Final Joy

Giovanni de Medici is an embarrassment to the Catholic Church. He became Pope Leo X in 1513 when he was thirty-eight years old. He had been a cardinal since he was thirteen. Like all his relatives in the wealthy but debauched de Medici clan, he loved pleasure. When elected pope, he is reported to have said, "God has given us the papacy; let us enjoy it!" He was lavish in his patronage of the arts; the most famous recipient of his largesse was the artist Raphael. *The Catholic Encyclopedia* describes him as "fat, shiny, effeminate," with a love of bawdy jokes and buffoonery. He loved Mardi Gras, and during Carnival season he went to a lot of balls, concerts, theatrical performances, and races. In short, he sounds like a man who would do well in New Orleans. A y'at, in speaking of his cherished religious faith, might paraphrase Leo X's slogan as "God has given New Orleans Catholicism; let us enjoy it!"

Hurricane Katrina

On August 29, 2005, New Orleans was changed forever by the largest natural disaster to hit the United States. Hurricane Katrina pushed water into Lake Pontchartrain until the flood walls and levees in several drainage canals ruptured, spilling billions of gallons of water into the city. Eighty percent of New Orleans was under water, and thousands of residents were trapped in their homes as the water rose higher. Thousands were rescued by boats and helicopters, then evacuated to places many had barely heard of. Suddenly New Orleans, a city of gaiety and charm was a filthy, broken ghost town, with a population of mostly emergency workers left searching for and coaxing out those who remained behind. They also began to remove corpses, eventually counting more than one thousand dead victims of the storm and flood in the city and surrounding parishes. The stench of death permeated the devastation.

The Archdiocese of New Orleans experienced damage, some of it severe, to hundreds of the structures it owns, including churches and schools. Notre Dame Seminary was flooded, and faculty and students escaped to St. Joseph's Abbey at St. Benedict, near Covington on the north shore. Auxiliary Bishop Roger Morin lost his home when a fire raged out of control during the flood and destroyed almost an entire square block. Hundreds of thousands of New Orleanians lost their homes, their businesses, and members of their families. Months after the storm had passed and the flood waters had been removed, there were still thousands of people unaccounted for and missing.

New Orleanians and Americans generally began to question why God had wrought his wrath so terribly on their homes, their city, and the Gulf Coast. Why did Our Lady of Prompt Succor not protect the city, they wondered. Some evangelical ministers and some Catholic priests as well spoke publicly of the Lord's punishment for sins of greed and the flesh, referring to the booming gambling industry or the laissez-faire attitude toward sexuality, especially homosexuality. Yet, these ministers, so secure in their knowledge of how God chooses to take retributive action, were at a loss to explain why so many innocent people were harmed, made homeless, or killed by a vengeful divinity.

Fortunately, most Catholic and Protestant clergy know better and explained that people of the area were not being punished and that those who claim to have direct communication with God do not know what they are talking about. The tragedy of Katrina provided the opportunity for New Orleanians and those who care throughout the country to express their sense of shared community, of responding positively and physically to Jesus' commandment to love one another. The outpouring of support from all over the world for the victims was inspiring.

Weeks after the storm, while the city of New Orleans

was still in darkness because of damaged electric power equipment, President George W. Bush came to Jackson Square to pledge the federal government's full support. "We cannot imagine an America without New Orleans," he said, with the facade of St. Louis Cathedral illuminated behind him by portable lighting and generating equipment. "New Orleans will rise again," he promised, inadvertently or deliberately using a metaphor from the New Testament. The city will rise again. Jesus rose after being battered and tortured, maimed and killed. He was a different person after resurrection, glorious and triumphant. New Orleans, too, can rise again, glorious and triumphant.

In the dark, in the stench, and in the waves of despair, St. Louis, patron saint of the city and the state, may have been looking down from the spires of his cathedral, which symbolizes the soul of this great city. Despite the mind-numbing breadth of Katrina's devastation, The Cathedral was spared, losing only a few shingles and some other minor damage. St. Louis would be pleased that the parochial grade school connected to The Cathedral was the first school on the east bank of New Orleans to reopen after Katrina. The nuns were again in the classroom teaching children, just as they have been doing for 278 years. Mass was again being celebrated in The Cathedral. St. Louis may be thinking that it is time for another great crusade. This new crusade will not be to rescue far-off Jerusalem, but to rescue New Orleans, holy to its inhabitants. This is a crusade that must not fail.

The St. Louis Cathedral was erected to resurrect New Orleans from its first terrible disaster, the Great Fire of Good Friday 1788. For more than two hundred and ten years, it has stood as a symbol of the persistence of the city, its people, and the Catholic faith that is such an integral part of their lives. It is now a beacon of inspiration to all who participate in rebuilding to combine their faith and prayer with hard work.

New Orleans will prevail. After all, God is a y'at.